Sewing
Tiny Toys

Carolyn Vosburg Hall

Krause Publications
700 E. State Street
Iola, WI 54990-0001
715-445-2214
www.krause.com

Please call or write for our free catalog of publications. Our toll-free number to place an order or obtain a free catalog is 800-258-0929 or please use our regular business telephone 715-445-2214 for editorial comment and further information.

Library of Congress Catalog Number 99-61443
ISBN 0-87341-787-9

The following products and companies appear in this publication:
Beanie Babies®
Darice Foamies® plastic sheets
FrayChek®
Gingher® scissors
Velcro® Brand

All photos, drawings, and designs by Carolyn Vosburg Hall

▲ *Emily and Ian Goodrich, bosses of their world, make these Tiny Toys toe the line as they play on the Sarasota beach.*

Acknowledgments

Thanks to: Claudia, Hattie, and Bradley Stroud for Tiny Toy names, to Hattie for ideas, and Bradley for a photograph. Thanks to these human models for posing: Cap Hall, Ross Hall, Ian and Emily Goodrich, Etsuko Sato Vosburg and Robert Hueter; and animals: former family pets, residents of the Detroit Zoo, and visiting creatures in our backyards. Thanks to my parents for teaching me the joys of making toys. And thanks to my editor, Amy Tincher-Durik, and designer, Jan Wojtech, for making the book look so good.

Table of Contents

Introduction

➤ *This 5" tall felt parrot is perched in an orange tree.*

Toys are a child's tools for learning about the world. They carry a certain magic, especially when they are homemade. Toys stir the imagination and delight the child in us. Even as a grandmother, I still find toys fascinating. The first toy I remember making, with Mom's help on the sewing machine, was a rag doll cut from Dad's old shirt. I still have that funny little rag doll I made more than half a century ago. Since then I've created hundreds of toys. Some were for my children, grandchildren, nephews, and others. Many toys and patterns were designed for my books Teddy Bear Craft Book (Prentice Hall) and The A to Z of Soft Animals (Prentice Hall) and for magazines such as Woman's Day, Threads, 1001 Good Ideas, and Southern Living. And some toys were designed for art exhibitions and my art book Soft Sculpture (Davis Publications).

▲ *Small children like small toys that fit easily in hand. Grandson Ross Hall looks over the Tiny Toy collection to make his choice.*

➤ *Bits of fabric, sewing supplies, and a little time are all that's needed to sew small toys.*

In this book, I've designed a zoo full of fifty-two small toy patterns for you to make (I designed more, but some of the toys only make cameo appearances). The first pattern, Tiny Teddy (page 14), started this collection. Based on the traditional 1903 teddy bear design, the toy is a 3" tall jointed bear made from felt and sewn by hand. You can hand-sew the toy in an hour or so. Switch colors to black and white to make a Panda (page 17) with a few pattern changes. Or you can rev up your sewing machine to stitch the Bunny (page 19) in even less time.

Toys in the book are arranged by how they are made. Half of them have moveable arms and legs, the better to perform their many roles as toys, party favors, package decorations, Christmas tree ornaments, mementos, or whatever you can imagine. (Watch for the many "Have You Thought of This?" sidebars contained in this book for ideas.) Some toys have armatures to stiffen long narrow arms, legs, or necks. Several toys are embellished by embroidery, appliqué, or paint. Decorative fabrics are introduced with information on how to sew them. Many toys have shifting stuffing to give a lifelike feel and appearance as they fall into poses similar to the popular Beanie Babies. Most of these have a combination of firm

and shifting stuffing to maintain shape. In the last section, patterns from the simple Starfish (page 116) to the complicated Dragon (page 141) show step-by-step how 3-D toy-making works. From this you can create your own patterns for small toys.

Anyone with basic sewing skills can make these toys by hand or sewing machine. All you need are nimble fingers and a dollop of patience to work with small pieces. Helpful hints about hand and machine sewing, stitches and threads, kinds of seams and types of fabrics, stuffings, and more is threaded throughout the book.

None of these patterns takes more than a square foot of fabric or takes *forever* to make. Tuck one in your purse or pocket to work on while waiting for the dentist or watching TV. These portable projects can be good for adults and children to sew together.

Carolyn Vosburg Hall

Sewing Felt Toys

Chapter 1

Tiny Toy Making Techniques

Toy Construction

Tiny toys, with moveable joints like a traditional teddy bear, must be firmly stuffed for the joint to work well. Tiny joints can be hinged on thread but larger ones will benefit from button disk joints. Details for making both joints appear on pages 26 and 27. Small floppy toys made from furry fabrics need a combination of stable and shifting stuffings (see pages 9 and 83). Because these toys are all small, they must be constructed in a certain order to cope with tiny seams, as described and shown in each pattern. Your toys may have a slightly different shape from those shown such as thinner legs, wider bodies, or formless heads. This depends on such factors as fabric stretch and flexibility, pattern cutting, and seam allowance sewing. You can make adjustments as you sew, or cut a new piece because so little is required.

Toy Patterns

The full-size patterns contained in this book list the number of pieces to cut, the color of felt or fabric to use, and construction information. Templates, patterns with no seam allowances, are intended for non-fraying fabrics like felt. Other patterns include a seam allowance, which can be added to templates. Use a tailor's pencil to trace the pattern pieces on fabric, especially with light-colored pieces. Don't be tempted to use a pen because it may discolor the exposed seams or bleed.

The success of these tiny figures depends on accurate cutting, so use sharp scissors and great care. For felt, cut exactly on the cutting line just inside your traced line. For fabric, cut on the seam allowance line. Cut each piece separately for accuracy. Cut pieces and trim the edges so they will match when seamed, especially for machine sewing. If pieces don't match exactly, place a pin at each end of the seam and ease the pieces to match as you sew.

▲ Many felt toys have firmly-stuffed bodies and moveable joints like old china (porcelain) dolls and early teddy bears. For making this joint, see page 14 (Tiny Teddy) and page 46 (Astronaut).

Here are some general pattern guidelines:

1. **Dot dash**: Indicates fold.

2. **Cut on fold**: Make a full unfolded pattern in paper. Cut all fabrics singly for accuracy.

3. **Dotted line**: The stitch line to whip-stitch or machine sew.

4. **Cut 2, 1 reversed**: For fabrics with a face and wrong side.

5. **Cut whole piece** and **Cut to here**: Indicate a larger pattern piece overlaps a smaller. Cut both as arrows show.

6. **No dotted line**: A template for felt. Add 1/8" or more seam allowances for fabric.

7. **Clip**: After machine sewing, clip seam allowance to the stitch line to decrease pull.

8. **Diagonal lines**: Wrong side of fabric.

9. **Join**: Another piece joins here.

10. **C to D**: In sewing, leave open to turn and stuff.

11. **Drawn lines**: Embroidery or eye insert.

12. **Ease**: Make a piece fit the adjoining one by pinning each end and sew.

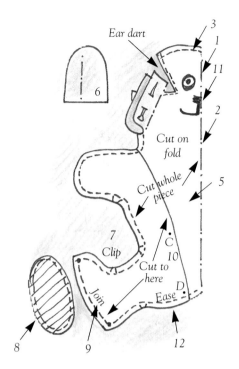

▲ *Some handy supplies: Assorted fabrics from faux fur to felt and metallics to animals prints, plastic sheets (black center) for hooves, furry pipe cleaners for horns and armatures, embroidery floss for faces, and plastic eyes or glass beads for eyes and noses.*

Toy Fabric

For small toys, use tightly-woven knitted or felt fabrics. Template patterns are designed for felt whether sewn right or wrong side out. For other fabrics, add a 1/8" (or more) seam allowance and sew from the reverse side. Do not use thick or loosely-woven fabrics because they will fray and pull out when stuffed. Furry fabrics add bulk to patterns like the Starfish (see page 22). The length of the nap and the stretch and firmness of the fabric will affect the shape of the toy. Each pattern recommends certain fabrics.

Stuffings

The primary stuffing of choice is polyester fiberfill. It mimics cotton, wool, kapok, and other fibers but is easier to use. This commonly available synthetic stuffing is extruded like silk in a monofilament fiber. It is washable, non-allergenic, and fairly inexpensive. It can be hard packed as needed for a jointed toy or loosely packed for a softer one. Packed softly, fiberfill will maintain its springy loft, but packed hard, it can become quite stiff. To stuff a toy, think like a sculptor and keep poking in bits of fiberfill to mold the shape. Use your sewing machine screw driver, a bamboo skewer, or a dowel rod to begin pushing small wads into the nose, head, and feet. Hold the toy in the palm of your hand so the seams will open but not pull out as you stuff. Jointed toys need hard stuffing so they can pivot properly.

All of the toys in Chapter 6, except the Lamb, are filled with fiberfill. The rest use polypropylene pellets which are relatively new on the market. They take the place of other heavier stuffings such as beans or sand. Pellet or granular stuffing shifts when not too fully packed, giving the toys a lifelike feel. You can use a funnel to pour in the pellets. You will find that even floppy toys need non-shifting stuffing in the heads and feet before pouring in the shifting pellets. More about stuffing appears in Chapter 6.

▲ *The best stuffing to use: 1. Polyester fiberfill (shown) is washable, inexpensive, and easy to use to make soft or firm toys. You can also use cotton, wool, other fiber, or excelsior (wood shavings) or cut up plastic bags. Use a wooden rod or screw driver to stuff. 2. Polypropylene pellets (shown) make a heavy shifting stuffing like old beanbags. Lacking this you could use dried beans, lentils, macaroni, or sand (with a tightly-woven fabric). Use a funnel to fill the toy and work over a pan to catch overflow. 3. Bamboo skewers help push in stuffing or act as armatures for narrow toy parts.*

▲ *Toy-making tools to keep on hand include: (upper left) needle-nosed pliers to pull needles through tough fabric or bend wires, good sharp scissors (Gingher knife-blade shown), small embroidery scissors (hook-nosed for clipping threads), kitchen scissors for cutting pipe cleaners, a magnetic pin holder, and pins (1-1/2" quilting pins shown; smaller silk pins are ideal).*

Turning

All patterns indicate leaving a seam open to turn and stuff, marked C to D for consistency's sake. To turn toys right side out, first poke the turning tool into the piece to open it. Avoid using sharp scissor tips or knitting needles to turn and stuff because they may poke holes. Your sewing machine screw driver, a bamboo skewer, or a dowel rod can better catch the stuffing to pack it in later. Poke the fabric at the toy's distant end inward to make a dent. From the outside, push the tool into the dent and carefully work the dent toward the opening. Be careful not to get a wadded up lump that won't budge. Keep pushing gently with the tool. Turn legs after the body is turned, using the tool to gently prod them out.

Threads

Thread shows on stuffed toy seams, so match the thread colors to the felt or fabric. Use sturdy threads such as polyester-coated cotton for seams. Hand sewing with quilting thread avoids tangles. Use even stronger thread for joints and embroidery floss for faces.

Each toy requires a different color thread, and some require more than one color. For this reason, it is easiest and most efficient to use several needles, each threaded with its own color. Thread colors are listed in each pattern and sometimes abbreviated by one or two of their first letters where this is necessary.

Sewing Seams

On felt toys, you can hand sew from the right side using a tiny whip-stitch about 1/8" long and sewn 1/8" into the fabric. When firmly stuffed, the seams open and flatten. Whip-stitching pulled tightly will shorten the seam length, which is useful in modeling the toy. Machine whip-stitching—zigzag stitching over the edges of joined pieces—causes seams to stretch slightly. Sewing seams from the reverse side requires the use of seam allowances to achieve the right shapes. See Useful Stitches on the next page.

Faces

The face you embroider on a toy adds personality. Aim to be as consistent with the original animal as possible for the best effect. Use the embroidery lines marked on the pattern coupled with the photograph of the toy as guides to create the face. Eyes carry the soul of these little characters so choose and place them carefully. Craft stores sell toy plastic eyes with a post and washer or a screw post and nut for larger animals. Eyes come in several colors and sizes, but few small enough for most of these toys. Various-sized glass or plastic beads are specified in most patterns. Sew these beads on firmly and place glue under them for added security. If the toys are for small children, embroider the eyes and sew the jointed legs on so firmly that they can't come off.

Each toy pattern and photo tells specifics on the faces. Generally, the face is hand-embroidered on the completed and stuffed toy using embroidery floss. Your aim is to avoid visible knots on your small toy. To hide the end of the thread, sew into the Head from a seam emerging at the Eye. Sew a knot (page 12), join one Eye bead, sew through the Head to the opposite Eye, and back to the first Eye. This anchors the Head stuffing and allows for pulling the thread firmly to seat the Eye beads. To secure, sew a second knot under the Eye bead. Insert the thread under the Eye and emerge at the Nose center. You can satin-stitch or sew on beads for the Nose. On certain animals, sew a stitch down from the Nose and emerge at the Mouth corner. Sew across the Muzzle, under the Nose thread, and into the other side of the Mouth. Sew the Mouth double, sew a knot at one corner of the Mouth, and sew back into the Head. Emerge at a seam and clip the thread. Only this last knot shows—no thread ends do.

Useful Stitches

Small-sized toys are most easily sewn by hand, but if you can control your sewing machine well, use it. Shown here are some stitches and seams you can use for sewing Tiny Toys by machine. For example, the Bunny was sewn by machine using a narrow zigzag stitch shown on the left, and the Kangaroo was sewn by machine with a short straight stitch and very narrow seam allowances.

No. 1 and No. 2 in the photo (from the left) show the seam pulled open to nearly flat. **No. 4** shows the horizontal stitches on the back of zigzag stitching. **No. 3** is a narrow satin-stitch used for surface embroidery or exposed decorative seams used on the Starfish (page 21).

No. 5 is a machine-sewn pin tuck used on the Armadillo (page 108). To do this, fold the fabric and sew along the edge.

No. 6 shows short-length straight machine stitching, sewn on the reverse side used for most shifting stuffing toys. **No. 7** shows this seam with edges exposed.

No. 8 shows the whip-stitch used for most felt toys. Sew it by matching edges back to back and insert the needle 1/8" from the edge, pull the thread through to the front, and pull tightly to seat the thread. Carry the thread over the seam edge and insert the needle in the back, 1/8" from the previous stitch. Whip-stitch over the edge firmly. An even rhythm will develop naturally.

Use strong, good-quality threads because the stitching must be pulled firmly on the seams. Polyester-cotton thread will probably work the best; quilting thread snarls and tangles less than most. Most fabrics require sewing from the reverse side and turning. The final seam is always sewn by hand from the right side of the fabric, because machine sewing a stuffed shape is difficult, if not impossible.

▲ Useful stitches (left to right on felt): machine zigzag overcast from the front, satin-stitch top-stitching, back side of machine overcast stitching, pin tuck (fold as fabric, sew near edge, and open flat), back side of machine straight-stitch seam, front of machine straight stitch seam 1/8" wide, hand sewn whip-stitching (fold fabric and whip stitch over edges), and hand whip-stitch as pulled open by stuffing.

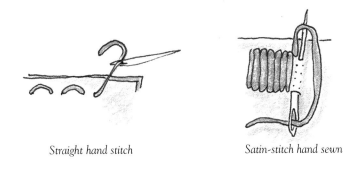

Straight hand stitch

Satin-stitch hand sewn

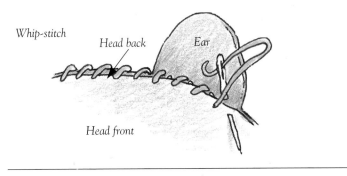

Whip-stitch

Head back

Ear

Head front

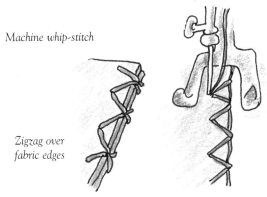

Machine whip-stitch

Zigzag over fabric edges

Knots

Beginning knot (Fig. 1 and 2): To begin, thread the needle and knot the doubled thread end. Sew into the fabric and back, open the threads in front of the knot, sew through, and pull to knot. This knot cannot pull out.

Finishing knot (Fig. 3): Sew a 1/8" stitch in the fabric, emerging at the thread. Pull to form a small loop, sew through the loop once or twice as needed, and pull tightly. Use this knot on the reverse side to begin or on the right side if necessary to end a seam. To conceal the thread tail, sew back into the felt at the base of the sewn knot emerging 1/2" or so away, pull to tighten, and clip off the thread.

French knot (Fig. 4): Nostrils and eyes can be sewn with French knots, using two or three strands of embroidery floss. Sew a knot to anchor the thread emerging on the right side. Aim the needle in the direction of the thread and twist the thread around it three or four times. Insert the needle at the thread, pinch the twist, and pull the needle through. A knot will form.

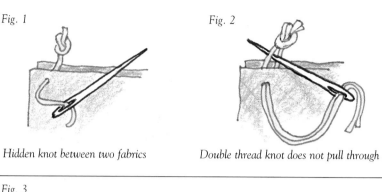

Fig. 1
Hidden knot between two fabrics

Fig. 2
Double thread knot does not pull through

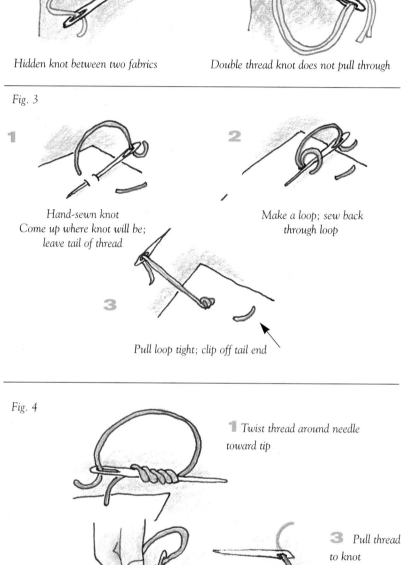

Fig. 3

1 *Hand-sewn knot*
Come up where knot will be; leave tail of thread

2 *Make a loop; sew back through loop*

3 *Pull loop tight; clip off tail end*

Fig. 4

1 *Twist thread around needle toward tip*

2 *Pull thread to tighten; sew back into fabric next to first hole*

3 *Pull thread to knot*

About Teddy Bears

As children, my sister and I loved our teddy bears. We named her large bear Big Teddy and mine Little Teddy after our Big Grandpa, a tall painter, and Little Grandpa, a regular-sized farmer. Early teddies, like my sister's Big Teddy, had hard-stuffed bodies and disk-jointed arms and legs. Little Teddy—who was tattered when I found him—leaked sawdust and lacked glass eyes. Watching my mother patch Little Teddy with buttons for eyes and a silk flower petal for an ear probably led to my love for sewing toys. This first pattern, on the next page, makes an even smaller Little Teddy, Tiny Teddy.

Making Big Teddy requires eight pattern pieces and fifteen cut-out pieces. A jointed Tiny Teddy, made of fifteen tiny pieces, would require nimble fingers indeed for such intricacy. So pattern pieces were overlapped, reworked, and joined to eliminate as many seams as possible—as were all of the patterns in the book. Tiny Teddy has four pattern pieces and eight cut-out pieces. He's made of felt, which eliminates seam allowances and the need to turn small pieces. This toy requires little fabric and little time to sew.

▲ *Tiny Teddy, at 3" tall, is six times smaller than the 18" Teddy made from my book* The Teddy Bear Craft Book *(Prentice Hall, 1983).*

1

Tiny Teddy

This makes a 3" tall teddy bear. You can use this pattern as a detailed guide for sewing other jointed toys. The template pattern shows typical construction. It is designed for felt to be sewn from the right or wrong side. For other fabric, add seam allowances and sew from the reverse side.

For a more bear-like animal, use the Brown Bear or the Polar Bear pattern (pages 100 and 135, respectively).

▲ *The teddy is a cuddly toy*
Just made to love a girl or boy.

Materials

Body, Arms, and Legs: 4" x 8" tan felt
Paws, Muzzle, and Feet: 1" x 2" cream felt
Fiberfill stuffing
Matching tan (T) thread, black (B) embroidery floss, and strong tan thread for joints

Eyes: Two 1/8" black beads
Ribbon: 9" of 1/8" wide ribbon
Sharp scissors, sewing needle, stuffing tool, Tacky Glue, pencil

1. Pattern: This template pattern has no seam allowances. Trace the template pieces carefully with a pencil or pin the template on the fabric and cut around it. Do not cut double because small pieces of felt may shift. Cut out all pieces exactly on the cutting line. If fabrics other than felt are used, add 1/8" seam allowances. Use only tightly-woven or knitted stable fabrics. Do not use thick or loosely-woven fabrics because they will fray and pull out when stuffed.

2. Body: Align the two Body pieces. Firmly whip-stitch the front and back seams from B to A or zigzag machine stitch 1/16" to 1/8" from the edge. For felt, stitch on the right side and pull seams open to stuff.

2. Bodies

3. Head: Match the Head dart from seam to seam and whip-stitch with the Ears remaining outside. If you stitch on the wrong side, be sure the Ears are out. For contrasting ear color, sew the Ear color to Ear front and continue as above.

3. Head/Ears

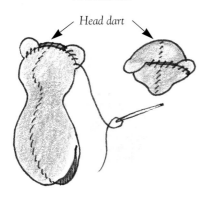

Head dart

4. Body: Push a ball of stuffing into the Nose to keep it firm. Stuff the toy with fiberfill bit by bit (so it feels as firm as your fingernail). Use small wads and "sculpture" the shape as you add each wad. Hold the bear as you stuff so the seams flatten a bit but do not pull apart. Align the Body dart seams and whip-stitch closed.

4. and 5.

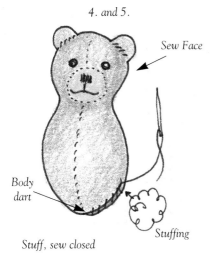

Sew Face

Body dart

Stuffing

Stuff, sew closed

5. Face:
A. Muzzle: If a contrasting muzzle is used, fold the Muzzle and sew the chin seam closed. Whip-stitch the muzzle to the bear's face.
B. Nose and Mouth: Use black embroidery floss (two or three strands) and sew a knot at the Nose to begin. Satin-stitch four vertical stitches 1/8" long for the nose. To sew the Mouth, sew down from the nose 1/8" and emerge at one side of the mouth. Sew the Mouth stitch across, passing under the Nose stitch, and insert the needle in the other side to complete the Mouth. Emerge at the Eye and sew a knot.
C. Sew one Eye bead in place and emerge at the other Eye. Sew through the Eye bead and back to the first Eye. Pull the thread to seat the Eyes. Sew a hidden knot and tuck the thread by sewing behind the Eye emerging at the neck. Clip off the thread. Glue under the Eye bead in addition to sewing for security.

6. Arm: Whip-stitch the optional-colored Paw to the Arm. Fold the Arm and sew from the Paw to 1/2" from the end of the seam. Don't clip the thread. Stuff the arm firmly. Whip-stitch the seam closed. Repeat for the second arm.

6. Arm

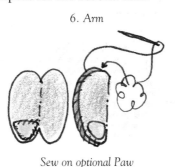

Sew on optional Paw

7. Leg: Fold the Leg and stitch from the top to the Foot. Don't clip the thread. Stuff the Leg firmly and align the Foot. Align and whip-stitch half of the Foot in place. Add more stuffing and continue to sew closed. Repeat for the other Leg.

7. Leg

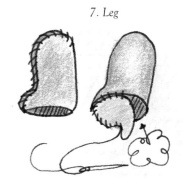

Sewn Joints

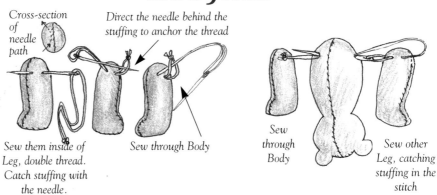

Cross-section of needle path

Direct the needle behind the stuffing to anchor the thread

8. Join Arms and Legs:
A. Using a strong double thread knotted at the end, insert the needle on the inside of the Arm at the top end, guide the needle around the stuffing, and emerge about 1/4" away from the insertion point. Sew through the knotted thread to secure and pull firmly.

B. Sew through the Body as marked. Sew the opposite inside Arm as above and sew back through the Body. Pinch the Arm joint firmly with your fingers and pull the thread until the Arms are firmly seated. Loop the thread around the Arm joint, sew through the loop, and pull carefully and firmly until a knot forms at the joint. Sew a second knot and clip the thread.

C. Repeat for the Legs.

9. Tie a bow knot ribbon at the Neck and clip off the ends.

Sew them inside of Leg, double thread. Catch stuffing with the needle.

Sew through Body

Sew through Body

Sew other Leg, catching stuffing in the stitch

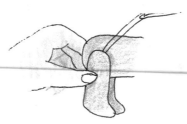

Pull thread to tighten joint; pinch

Sew a knot around the joint thread; sew through loop

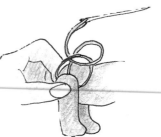

Pull tight to knot, sew second knot; clip threads

8. Joints
9. Ribbon

Strong thread

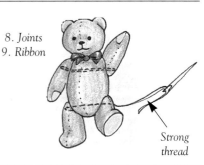

Tiny Teddy Pattern

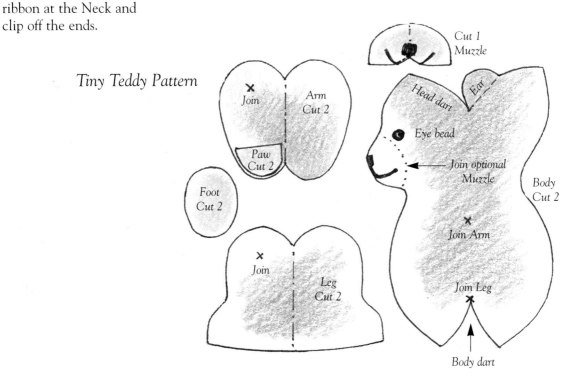

Cut 1
Muzzle

Join

Arm
Cut 2

Paw
Cut 2

Foot
Cut 2

Join

Leg
Cut 2

Head dart

Ear

Eye bead

Join optional Muzzle

Body
Cut 2

Join Arm

Join Leg

Body dart

Chang, the Panda

This pattern, similar to the Tiny Teddy pattern, adds another color to make a 3" tall panda. For more detail in instructions, see the Tiny Teddy pattern (pages 14-16). Because so many changes of thread color occur, this is best sewn by hand or with monofilament thread by machine.

Materials

Chest, Head, and Body: 3" x 4" white felt and 4" x 4" black felt
Paws: 1" x 2" gray felt
Fiberfill stuffing
Matching black (B) and white (W) thread and needle for each
Black embroidery floss, strong thread for joints
Eyes: Two 1/8" black beads
Needle, sharp scissors, stuffing tool

▲ *The panda wears black mitts and boots*
And only dines on bamboo shoots.

◄ *Grandson Ross Hall, like many little boys, stuffs little toys down his shirt.*

Have You Thought of This?

Tie the Panda, or any other toy, on a wrapped gift with a bow to increase the anticipation of finding goodies inside.

1. Pattern: Cut out all pattern pieces. For fabrics other than felt, add 1/8" seam allowances.

2. Body:

A. Align the Heads and sew the back seam (W).

B. Align the Chest pieces and sew the back seam (B).

C. Fold and sew the Tail (B).

D. Pin the Tail on the Body. Match Bodies and sew the back seam (W).

E. Open the pieces, sew the Head to the Chest, and the Chest to the Body (B).

F. Align the Body and sew the front seams: Head (W), Chest (B), and Body (W).

3. Head: Pin or baste the Ears in place. Match the Head dart edges and sew closed with Ears upright.

4. Stuff: Push fiberfill into the Nose, then fill the toy. Whip-stitch the Body dart closed.

5. Face: With the embroidery floss (two or three strands), sew the Nose and Mouth as shown, emerging at the Eye. Sew Eye bead on Eye patch, emerging at the other Eye, repeat, and sew a hidden knot under the Eye patch.

6. Fold the Arm or Leg. Sew to the end, stuff, and sew closed.

7. Joints: See Button Joints, page 26, or Sewn Joints, page 27.

*Insert Ears
Sew Head dart*

*Eye beads over
Eye patches*

*Stuff
Sew opening
closed*

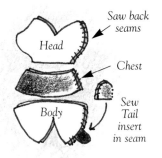

Saw back seams

Head

Chest

Body

Sew Tail insert in seam

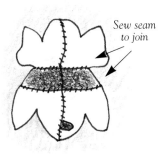

Sew seam to join

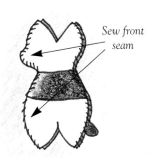

Sew front seam

Panda Pattern

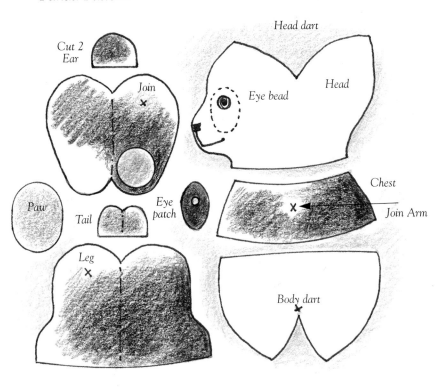

*Cut 2
Ear*

Join

Paw

Tail

Eye patch

Leg

Head dart

Eye bead

Head

Chest

Join Arm

Body dart

Bun Bun, the Bunny

This pattern makes a 5″ long bunny. Sewing Tiny Toys by hand is probably easier, but you can also sew them by machine. This toy was zigzag stitched by machine over the matched fabric edges by 1/8″.

▲ *Wild rabbits munch in our backyard*
But catching one is very hard.

Materials

Body, Arms, Legs, and Ear backs: 5″ x 9″ white felt
Ear fronts: 2″ x 2″ pink felt
Tail: 30″ white yarn
Ribbon: 10″ of 1/8″ pink ribbon
Fiberfill stuffing
Matching white thread

Sturdy white thread
Bright pink embroidery floss
Eyes: Two 1/8″ red beads
Sharp scissors, sewing machine or hand needle, stuffing tool

1. Pattern: Cut out all pattern pieces.

2. Body: Align the two Body pieces. Zigzag or whip-stitch from Ear slot to Ear slot, leaving C to D open. Use white thread for seams and sturdy white thread for the joint.

Set machine to narrow zigzag; sew
Leave C to D open

2.

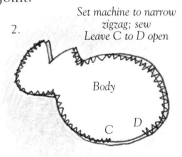

Body

C D

3. Ears: Align the pink Ear front and the white Ear back and sew the edges. Repeat. Fold the Ear, pink inside. Align the Ears in the Head dart, folded Ear edges touching, pink forward. Pin or baste.

Sew pink Ear to white Ear; fold

3.

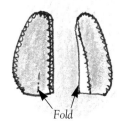

Fold

4. Head: Fold the Head dart over the Ears, edges aligned wrong side out, and sew with Ears upright.

Place folded Ears in Head dart wrong side out

4.

Sew across

5. Body: Stuff the bunny firmly with fiberfill. Sew C to D closed.

6. Face: For the Nose and Mouth, use the bright pink embroidery floss (two or three strands). To begin, sew a knot at the Eye and sew on the Eye bead, emerging at the opposite Eye. Repeat, emerging at the Nose. Sew two diagonal nose stitches and emerge at one side of the Mouth. Sew the Mouth stitch across under the Nose stitch and insert the needle in the other side, emerging at the Eye. Sew a hidden knot.

6.

*Ears,
Pink Eye beads,
pink Nose,
Mouth, ribbon*

7. Legs: Fold the Leg and sew from the Paw to 1/2" from the end of the seam. Stuff firmly and whip-stitch closed. Repeat for all Legs. Sew pink Paws.

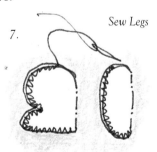

Sew Legs

7.

8. Tail: To make a pompom Tail, wrap white yarn around two fingers ten times. Wrap the strong thread around the yarn between your fingers, slide the yarn off, and tie a tight knot. Clip the loops evenly and use the dangling thread to sew on the Tail.

Wrap your pompom, tie string, clip ends even; sew on

Bunny Pattern

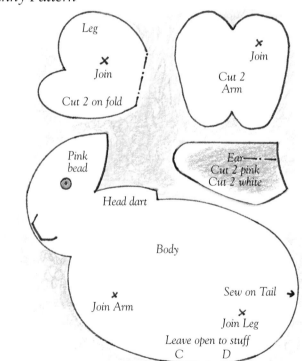

Leg

✗
Join

Cut 2 on fold

Pink bead

Head dart

Body

✗
Join Arm

Sew on Tail ➜

✗
Join Leg

Leave open to stuff
C   D

✗
Join

Cut 2
Arm

Ear — · —
Cut 2 pink
Cut 2 white

9. Finish: Join the Legs (described more fully on the Tiny Teddy and Astronaut, pages 14 and 46, respectively). Use strong double thread to sew into the Leg and back, through the Body into the opposite Leg and back. Sew through the body and pull the thread until the Legs are firmly seated, pinch the joint to hold it, and loop the thread around the Leg joint. Sew a double knot at the joint. Clip the thread. Repeat.

10. Tie a bow knot ribbon at the neck to finish and clip off the ends.

Have You Thought of This?

Easter baskets hidden on the lawn or behind a chair can include any number of small treasures: here are little stuffed toys, plastic eggs full of goodies, and a decorative Russian wooden egg.

Stella, Twinky, Sparkle, and Fuzz, the Starfish

▲ *Five arms or more on these small creatures*
Are quite distinguishable features!

The simple Starfish pattern, the same for each one pictured, shows how different fabrics look when sewn and stuffed. Patterns are usually designed for certain fabrics because they affect the construction, size, and appearance of a toy. Generally, Tiny Toys are designed for non-fraying fabrics with narrow seam allowances; other fabrics and means of construction give different results. These starfish show how this works.

This starfish is made of various fabrics and sewn in different ways to show how this affects the shape—all make a starfish from 4-1/2" to 5" across. From the left: 1. Hand-sewn felt with unturned seams and decorative machine stitching on top 2. Machine-sewn turned edges of decorative metallic knit fabric 3. Felt fabric satin-stitched on the edges unturned. 4. Faux fur with a 1/2" pile (fur length) machine sewn and turned.

Materials Noted for Each Fish:

Body: 5" x 10" felt, a decorative lightweight polyester knit with printed metallic design, felt, or a
furry fabric, as noted for each fish
Fiberfill stuffing or pellets

Matching or decorative threads
Sewing machine or hand sewing needle, turning tool
(i.e. small screw driver or bamboo skewer), sharp
scissors, funnel

How Felt Works for Toys

1. Starfish One is hand-sewn of felt with machine embroidery designs on top.

Felt is specified because it does not fray when cut and yet is flexible enough to mold to shape when stuffed. The narrow seams can be left unturned and exposed or turned for a finished look. Craft felt usually contains a mix of fibers, such as cotton and rayon, requiring an added adhesive to bind the fibers together. Medium-quality felt, usually a blend of wool and rayon or cotton, works best, because it is neither too heavy to be molded by the stuffing nor so thin that it pulls apart. If you can see light through the felt, it is probably too thin. Hat felt is too thick to flex enough.

Making Starfish One: Trace two patterns on felt. Set the sewing machine to the pattern you want and machine embroider a star pattern on one or both pattern pieces. Cut out both pieces on the seam line. Match the pieces back to back and begin to sew 1" from a tip. Whip-stitch both pieces together around the tip and all around to 3/4" from where you started. Use a stuffing tool to push bits of fiberfill into the Starfish until plump. Whip-stitch closed.

How Materials Affect Toys

2. Starfish Two is machine-sewn from the reverse side of a decorative fabric and turned.

Various fabrics and stuffings result in different shaped toys. Woven and knit fabrics require an added seam allowance because sewing subtracts edge fabric and makes the pattern area smaller. Some decorative fabrics—like this lightweight metallic/ polyester knit with a sequin pattern printed on—fray very little but do not leave a clean exposed edge. To look the best, they need to be sewn from the reverse side and turned. Choose firmly-woven, knitted, or felted fabrics that don't fray and add a narrow seam allowance. Other useable fabrics include tightly-woven cotton broadcloth, lightweight firmly woven wool, double-knit polyesters, knit-backed plush fabrics, suede cloth, fake furs, and other pile fabrics. Fiberfill makes a soft, light toy, and shifting pellet stuffing makes a floppy toy.

Making Starfish Two: Trace the pattern on paper. Fold fabric double face to face and pin on the paper pattern. The paper acts as both guide for sewing and stabilizer for shifting fabric. Set the sewing machine to a short-length stitch. Yes, you can machine sew through printed

sequins! Match the pieces face to face and begin to sew 1" from tip C. Sew around the tip (don't sew a sharp point) and continue around to 3/4" from where you started, D. Cut out the toy 1/8" from the stitch line and tear away the paper. Carefully turn the toy. Push a funnel into the opening and pour in pellets to suit or use fiberfill. Tuck in the raw edges and whip-stitch closed.

How Sewing Affects Toys

3. Starfish Three was machine-sewn right side out with a satin-stitch which forms a decorative border.

The way toys are sewn affects their shape. When pieces are whip-stitched together, the seam opens somewhat when stuffed, achieving close to a butt joint (meaning end to end). Done carefully, seams won't pull out. Whip-stitching flexes, with machine-sewn seams less so. When a stuffed shape plumps up, the edges wrinkle. Felt will adjust to this but firmly-woven fabrics cannot. See the Starfish (page 116) for coping with this. Here satin-stitching on the seam line stiffens the edge and helps hold the shape. It also adds a decorative touch.

Making Starfish Three: Trace two patterns on felt. Cut out both pieces on the seam line. Set the sewing machine to a short stitch-length medium-wide zigzag. Thread both top and bobbin with matching decorative thread. Match the pieces back to back and begin to sew 1" from a tip. Satin-stitch both pieces together around the tip and all around to 3/4" from where you started. Lightly stuff with fiberfill and satin-stitch closed. If the satin-stitch coverage isn't good, sew around again.

How Novelty Fabrics Affect Toys

4. Starfish Four is sewn wrong side out of furry fabric.

Sequined fabric makes a glittery toy, while fur fabric makes a fatter starfish and blurs the shape. For toy animals, the fur pile must be very short or the shape of the toy will be obscured. The length of the nap must be figured into the pattern. Some knit fabrics stretch—one way (across the width) or both ways (with elastic threads woven in)—which alters the toy's shape.

Making Starfish Four: Trace two patterns on the reverse side of the fur fabric, one reversed. Cut out both pieces with 1/8" seam allowances. Snip tiny stitches to avoid cutting the pile. Set the sewing machine to a short-length stitch. Match the pieces face to face and begin to sew 1" from tip C. Tuck the pile into the seam with a long pin as you sew. Sew around the tip (don't sew a sharp point) and continue around to 3/4" from where you started, D. Use a tool to carefully turn the toy. Insert a funnel in the opening and pour in pellets. Tuck in raw edges and whip-stitch closed. If pile is caught in the seam, pick it out gently with a long pin.

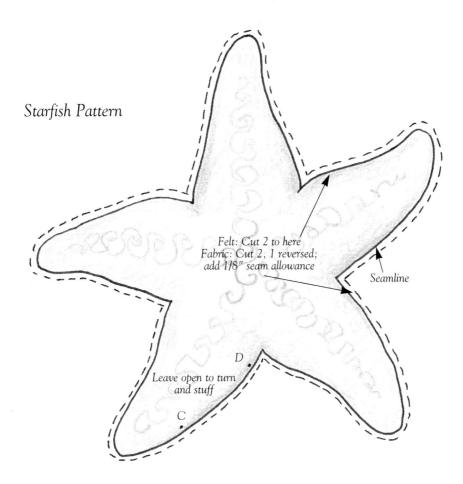

Starfish Pattern

Felt: Cut 2 to here
Fabric: Cut 2, 1 reversed;
add 1/8" seam allowance

Seamline

D

*Leave open to turn
and stuff*

C

Chapter 2

Jointed Felt Toys

China dolls were popular a hundred years ago and set the standard for some of today's toys. The stiff doll bodies made of porcelain achieved movement of the arms and sometimes legs with limbs strung together on elastic or wire. Hard-stuffed toys can have joints that swivel around a thread or, in larger toys, swivel on disks joined with a cotter pin. (Softly-stuffed toy joints don't move but can flex.) Here are two ways to make hard-stuffed toy joints:

Button Joints

1. The Cow's Leg (page 28): A button sewn into the Leg makes a sturdy joint that holds firmly to the Body. Teddy disk joints are held together with cotter pins, but here a strong thread suffices. Choose a button just smaller than the top of the Arm or Leg.

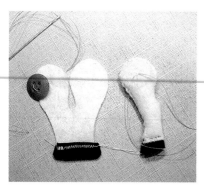

2. Use sturdy thread to sew through the inside of the Leg fabric into the button holes. Sew back through a different hole and the inside Leg fabric. Leave 6" tails on each end of the thread for tying later. Notice the Hoof is sewn on first.

3. Fold to align the Leg edges and hand-sew the Leg seam. To make sure the button lies flat to the fabric, sew the top of the Leg and stuff it.

4. Finish sewing the Leg seam. Use a stuffing tool such as your sewing machine screw driver to poke stuffing in. Sew across the Ankle to close. Note the thread tails.

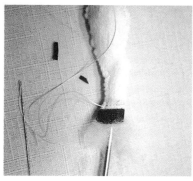

5. When the Body is sewn and stuffed, thread the 6" tails on one Leg, position it on the Body and sew through to the other side. Leave the threads dangle.

6. Rethread the tails on the other Leg and sew through the Body in the same hole as the opposite Leg. Pinch the joint and pull on these threads to tighten the joint. Tie a double or triple knot around the threads from the opposite side at this joint. Pull the opposite side thread tails firmly and double knot to complete the joint.

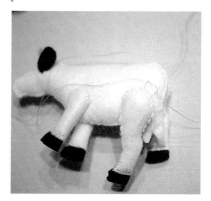

Sewn Joints

1. This 4" Astronaut (page 46), has hand-sewn joints because his Arms and Legs are too small for button joints. The following directions show how to sew this joint, a slight variation on the Tiny Teddy sewn joint (see page 16).

2. First, sew the boot to the Leg. Choose a strong, durable thread. Knot the doubled thread. Fold and sew the Leg seam wrong side out. Turn and sew the Foot in place, stuffing the Leg before you close the seam. Sew into the Leg inside top, guiding the needle around the stuffing and out the other side. Sew back through the same hole, guiding the needle around the stuffing on the other side and out the entry hole. Sew through the knot and pull firmly to secure. The

fabric may dimple on the outside. To avoid the dimple, see the Tiny Teddy sewn joint (page 16).

3. Sew the Body wrong side out, turn, stuff, and sew closed. To join the Leg, sew through the Body and out the other side.

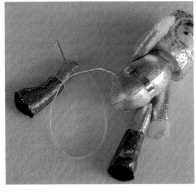

4. Sew through the opposite Leg from the inside as described above. Guide the needle tip around the stuffing, out the other side, and back around the stuffing. With luck or skill, you can sew back into the Leg entering the same hole, go around the stuffing, and pull the thread through the fabric into the Leg with the thread looping the stuffing. This way, no dimple shows.

5. Sew back through the body, emerging at the same entry hole.

6. Pinch the joint to compress the stuffing and pull on the thread to seat the legs tightly. Loop the thread around the joint. Still pinching the joint, sew through the loop to form a knot and pull firmly to knot.

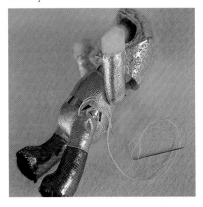

7. Sew a second knot around the joint, pull tightly to set the knot, and clip off the threads.

5

Cassie, the Cow

This makes a 5" long cow. You can appliqué, glue, or paint spots on the cow.

► *The Guernsey cow will call out "Moo"*
When she has some milk for you.

Materials

Body: 6" x 9" white felt (or desired color; add 1/8"
    seam allowance for other fabric)
Nose and Bag: 2" x 3" pink or flesh felt (add 1/8"
    seam allowance for other fabric)
Hooves: 1-1/2" x 2" black felt or foam sheet*
Eyes: Two black beads
Horns: 3" tan pipe cleaner

Button joints: Two 5/8" buttons and two 3/8"
    buttons
White (W) thread, black (B) thread, strong thread for
    joints
Polyester stuffing
Black felt for spots or black acrylic paint and brush
Scissors, craft scissors, needles, screwdriver
Darice Foamies were used in this project

1. Pattern: Cut out pattern pieces and randomly shaped spots.

2. Bag (the milk pouch is often called an udder bag): Lay the Bag on the Body face to face, sew and unfold. Repeat for the other side.

3. Body: Match the two Body pieces and sew from the Chin down the Neck to C. Sew from D to around the Bag (udders out) to the Tail mount.

4. Head:
A. Fold the Ear, tuck it fold-forward into the Ear dart, and pin. Fold dart over the Ear and sew. Repeat.
B. Sew the Nose to the Face. Align the Nose/Face to the

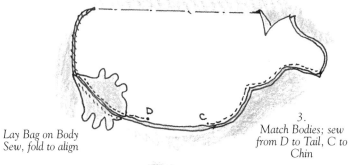

Lay Bag on Body
Sew, fold to align

3.
Match Bodies; sew
from D to Tail, C to
Chin

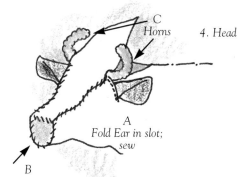

C
Horns

4. Head

A
Fold Ear in slot;
sew

B

Head and pin. Whip-stitch from the Ear dart to the Nose to other Ear dart.

C. Horns: Twist the pipe cleaner for Horns into an open figure-8 as shown. Tuck the loop into the Head. Pull the Head over the Horns, align to the Neck, and sew closed. Trim the Horn length.

D. Stuff the Head first, then pack the Body firmly. Sew the Body closed.

5. Legs:

A. Overlap the Leg on the Hoof 1/8" and satin-stitch. Repeat for all.

B. Make the Leg button joints as shown on page 26.

6. Spots, Eyes, Mouth, and Nose: (See Faces, page 10.) Use thread (B) to appliqué spots. Sew one Eye, emerge at the other Eye, and pull threads. Sew a knot. Sew the Nose and Mouth and emerge under a spot. Sew a knot and clip.

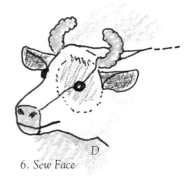

6. Sew Face

7. Tail: Clip felt ends to fringe and fold the Tail. Sew from the fringe up and join Tail to Body angled down (see above illustration).

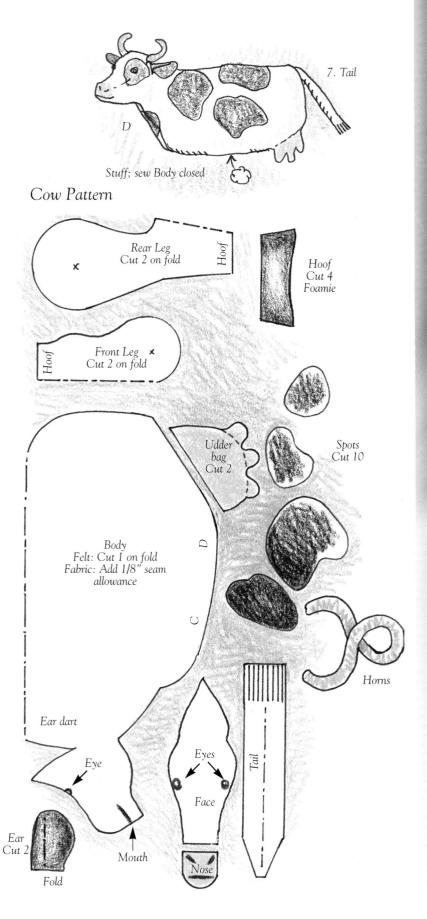

7. Tail

Stuff; sew Body closed

Cow Pattern

Rear Leg
Cut 2 on fold

Hoof

Hoof
Cut 4
Foamie

Front Leg
Cut 2 on fold

Hoof

Udder
bag
Cut 2

Spots
Cut 10

Body
Felt: Cut 1 on fold
Fabric: Add 1/8" seam
allowance

D

C

Horns

Ear dart

Eye

Tail

Eyes

Face

Ear
Cut 2

Fold

Mouth

Nose

6

Caravan, the Camel

This makes a 5" long camel. Camels helped invent felt. The best felt is made from wool, which, under heat, pressure, and movement, compacts into a tough non-woven fabric. Long ago you would toss a cushion of fleece under your sweaty camel's saddle and ride across the desert. The heat, moisture, and compression from the movement compacted the wool into felt. Crinkled wool fiber will mat like the fur on some long-haired cats or dogs.

▲ *The camel has a hump to ride*
And space for water kept inside.

Materials

Body: 6" x 9" tan felt
Eyes: Two black beads
Tan (T) thread, Black (B) thread, strong thread for
    joints

Polyester stuffing
Saddle: 3" x 6" decorative fabric
Sharp scissors, stuffing tool, needle

1. Pattern: Cut out pattern pieces.
2. Legs: To sew the Legs, see page 26 for Button Joints or page 27 for Sewn Joints.
3. Body: Match the Body pieces and sew from the Nose B down to C. Sew from D to the Head opening.

4. Sew Head dart: Fold and pin the Ears, with the fold forward. Align the Face to the Body at the Nose. Whip-stitch with the Ears sticking out.

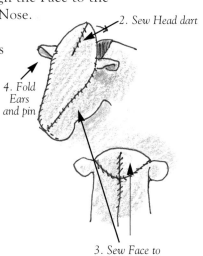

2. Sew Head dart

4. Fold Ears and pin

3. Sew Face to Head

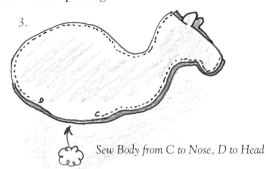

3.

Sew Body from C to Nose, D to Head

5. Begin at the Head to stuff firmly. Sew the opening closed C to D.

6. Face: Sew as shown on page 10.

7. Stuffing alters the pattern shape, so cut and sew the saddle to fit.

Stuff
Sew Nose, Mouth, Beads
for Eyes

Camel Pattern

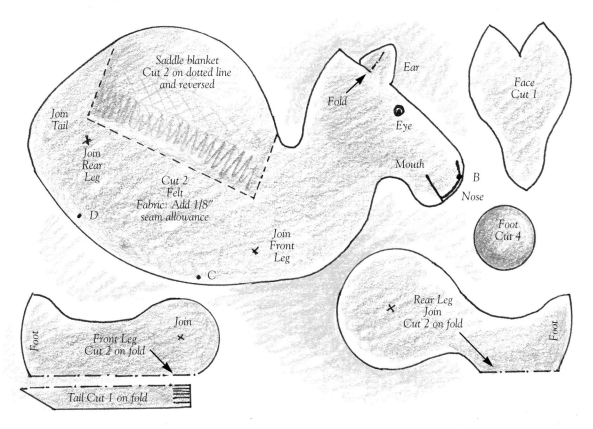

Saddle blanket
Cut 2 on dotted line
and reversed

Join
Tail

Join
Rear
Leg

Cut 2
Felt
Fabric: Add 1/8"
seam allowance

D

Join
Front
Leg

C

Ear

Fold

Eye

Mouth

B
Nose

Face
Cut 1

Foot
Cut 4

Foot

Front Leg
Cut 2 on fold

Join

Tail Cut 1 on fold

Rear Leg
Join
Cut 2 on fold

Foot

Foot

Ellie, the Elephant

This pattern makes a 4-1/4" tall elephant. Some of the fun of playing with toys is scale. Here's a huge elephant now the size of an orange. We can make the creatures of the world do our bidding in this tiny size. Toys spur the imagination.

▲ *A pachyderm big as a house*
Still is frightened by a mouse.

Materials

Head, Ears, Body, and Legs: 5" x 10" gray felt
Tusks: 1" x 2" white felt
Eyes: Two 1/8" black beads
Fiberfill stuffing

Gray (G) thread, white (W) thread, strong gray thread for joints
Sharp scissors, sewing needle, stuffing tool

1. Pattern: Cut out all pattern pieces.
2. Legs: To sew the Legs, see page 26 for Button Joints or page 27 for Sewn Joints.

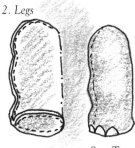

2. Legs

Fold, sew
Sew Foot   *Sew Toes*

3. Body:
A. Fold the Tusk and sew from the end to the top.
B. Pin the Tusk in Tusk slot, fold Head over, and sew from the reverse side. Repeat.

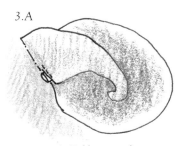

3.A

A. Fold, sew tusk
B. Fold Body over Tusk

C. Fold the Ear forward at the top as marked and pin. Fold the Ear dart over the Ear and sew from the reverse side. Repeat. Pin the Tail on.
D. Match Body pieces and whip-stitch the Body from C to the head. Stuff the Trunk. Continuing sewing to D, including the Tail.

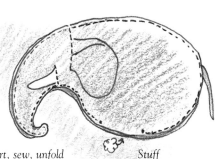

Stuff

C. Fold Body over Ear in Ear dart, sew, unfold
D. Sew Bodies together

4. Stuff firmly with fiberfill. Aim the Tusk and Ear seams back so Tusks face forward and Ears stick out. Whip-stitch the Body closed.

5. Face: Sew as shown. (See Faces, page 10, for instructions.)

Elephant Pattern

Tusk
Cut 2

Ear dart

Eye

Body
Felt: Cut 2

Tail

Tusk dart

Join Front Leg

Join Rear Leg

Tail
Cut 1

Leave open to stuff

Fold

Ear
Cut 2

Join

Front
Leg
Cut 2
on fold

Join

Rear
Leg
Cut 2
on fold

Foot
Cut 4

THE WALL STREET JOURNAL

What's News —

Have You Thought of This?

Guess who's a Republican! My husband, Cap Hall, models the latest in convention wear. For a Democratic donkey, substitute longer ears and a rope-like tufted tail on the Pony pattern (page 36).

8

Thistle, the Scotty Dog

This pattern makes a 4-1/4" dog. Sewing black on black is hard to see. If you use white stuffing, it may show if the seams pull apart in places. Mend these seams with black thread to strengthen them and hide the stuffing.

▲ Scotties have black fur that bristles
And they come when master whistles.

Materials

Body: 6" x 9" black felt
Fiberfill stuffing (black, if possible)
Matching black thread, strong black thread for joints

Eyes: Two 1/8" black beads
Ribbon: 12" of 1/2" wide plaid
Sharp scissors, sewing needle, stuffing tool

1. Pattern: Trace pattern on felt with a white pencil and cut out all pattern pieces.
2. Body: Fold the Body at the center Head to match Body sides. Sew from the Head dart to D.

3. Head:
A. Fold the Head dart, matching seams. Tuck the Ear base in the seam and sew across with the Ears upward.

B. Chin: Align the Nose to the Head and sew. Continue to sew this seam from the Chin to C.

4. Stuff: Stuff the Scotty very firmly, Tail and Nose first. Whip-stitch the Body seam closed.

5. Face: (See Faces, page 10.) Place the Eyebrow and sew on the Eye bead. Repeat and sew a knot. Emerge at the Nose and embroider or sew on beads. Sew a knot, hide the thread end, and clip off the thread.

6. Legs: To sew the Legs, see page 26 for Button Joints or page 27 for Sewn Joints.

7. Tie the plaid ribbon in a bow around the Neck.

Scotty Dog Pattern

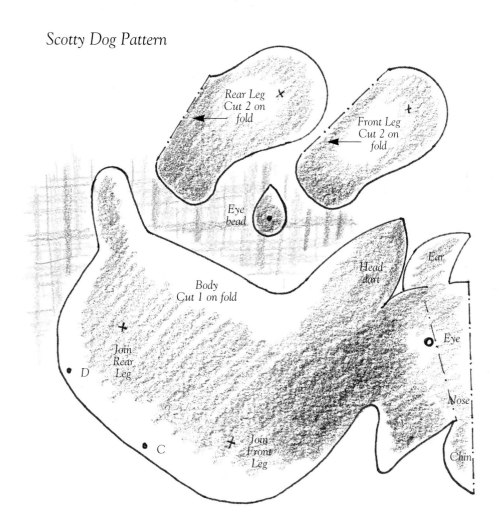

9

Oats, the Pony

This pattern makes a 4" tall pony. Make your pony any color you like—a tawny Palomino or a spotted Appaloosa. Or use the basic pattern to make a donkey (add longer ears, a rope-like tail, and a short bristly mane), a striped zebra (same changes), or a unicorn (white with a forehead horn).

▲ *Watch the circus pony prance. On her back trick riders dance.*

Materials

Body, Head, and Legs: 5" x 10" brown felt
Hooves: 1" x 2" tan felt
Saddle: 1-3/4" x 2-1/2" purple felt and pink felt strap
Tail: 1/2 oz. (about 3 yards) light-gold baby-size yarn
Eyes: Two 1/8" black beads

Trim for saddle blanket
Fiberfill stuffing
Matching thread, black embroidery floss, strong thread for joints
Sharp scissors, sewing needle, stuffing tool, ruler

1. Pattern: Cut out all pattern pieces.
2. Ears: Align the Ear slot with the Ears upright and sew from the reverse side with Ears outside. Repeat.

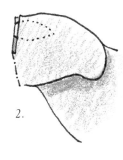

2.

3. Mane: Wrap a 1" wide ruler with the yarn thirty-four times to measure 1-3/4" wide. Align the wrapped ruler with one side of the Body Neck and whip-stitch the Mane to the Neck edge. Pull out the ruler. To machine-stitch, slide the yarn off the ruler and sew along one edge so the Mane measures 2" along the seam. Sew to the neck edge.

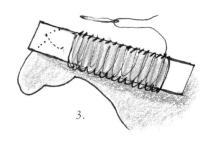

3.

4. Tail: Wrap the remaining yarn around three fingers five or six times. Tie a knot around the yarn and sew the knot to the Tail mount on the Body. Clip yarn ends.

4.

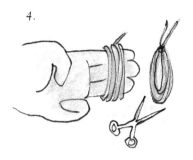

5. Muzzle: For a contrasting Muzzle, join the Muzzle to the Nose and whip-stitch.

6. Body: Align the two Body pieces, Tail and Mane out.

7. Stuff: Pack the pony very firmly with fiberfill, beginning with the Nose. Fill the Body, align the opening seams, and whip-stitch C to D closed.

8. Legs: To sew the Legs, see page 26 for Button Joints or page 27 for Sewn Joints. Sew on the hooves and stuff the legs.

9. Face: (See Faces, page 10.) Use the black embroidery floss to sew Nostril and Mouth. Sew on bead Eyes. Option: To make a Unicorn: Add a horn to the horse's forehead. Spiral-wrap the horn with a tight thread.

10. Saddle: Decorate the saddle with beading, sequins, ribbons, or as desired. Put on Saddle and sew the girth strap to the saddle.

8. to 11.

Pony Pattern

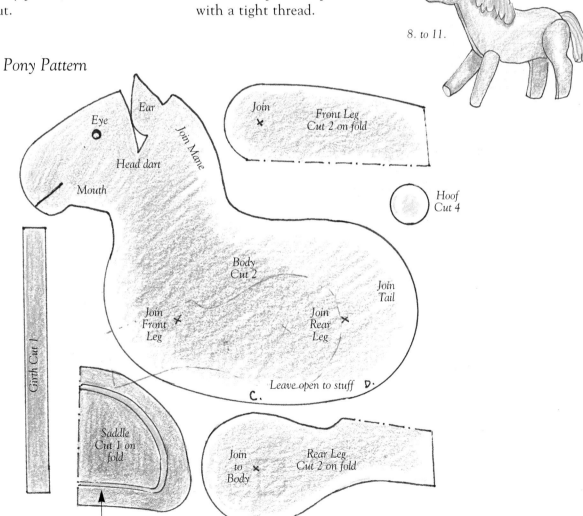

10

Oink, the Pig

This pattern makes a 3-1/2" pig (plus tail). The pig is machine-sewn with a narrow zigzag stitch over matched edges.

▲ *This little piggy made a house of brick*
And fooled the wolf with a clever trick.

Materials

Head, Body, and Legs: 4" x 8" pink felt
Eyes: Two 1/8" red beads
Fiberfill stuffing

Matching thread and deep pink embroidery floss
Sharp scissors, stuffing tool, needle, sewing
   machine (optional)

1. Pattern: Cut out all pattern pieces.
2. Ear: Align the Ear in the Head dart, fold dart over the Ear, and sew from the reverse side with the Ear outside. Repeat.

3. Body: Align the two Body pieces, matching the sewn Head darts. Whip-stitch around the Nose to D. Sew from the Chin to C.
4. Nose: Sew Nose to Body.
5. Stuff: Begin at the Nose to stuff the piggy firmly. Align the opening and whip-stitch closed.

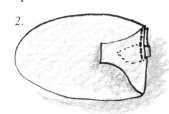

2.

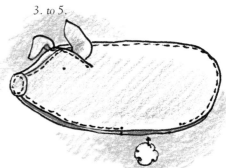

3. to 5.

6. Face: (See Faces, page 10.) Use the deep pink embroidery floss to sew French knots for the nostrils. Emerge at the Mouth side, sew the mouth, and sew a knot emerging at the Eye. Sew on a red Eye bead and emerge at the other Eye. Sew a hidden knot under the Eye.

7. Legs: To sew the Legs, see page 26 for Button Joints or page 27 for Sewn Joints. Fold the Leg lengthwise and sew from the top to the Foot. Stuff the Leg and sew closed.

8. Tail: Fold the Tail lengthwise and sew from the base to the end. Sew back through the stitches just sewn and pull the thread to curl the tail. Sew the Tail to the Body.

8.

6.

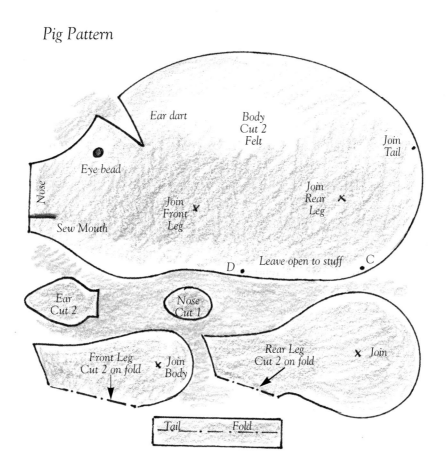

Pig Pattern

Ear dart

*Body
Cut 2
Felt*

*Join
Tail*

Eye bead

Nose

*Join
Rear
Leg*

*Join
Front
Leg*

Sew Mouth

Leave open to stuff

D   C

*Ear
Cut 2*

*Nose
Cut 1*

*Rear Leg
Cut 2 on fold*   *Join*

*Front Leg
Cut 2 on fold*   *Join
Body*

Tail   *Fold*

Chapter 3

Seams and Color Changes

A toy's shape comes mainly from the contours of pattern pieces. Sewing tiny complicated seams is difficult, so these toys are designed with the fewest possible seams (as mentioned in the Tiny Teddy pattern, page 14). Placement of these seams is important on toys as small as these; you don't want seams visibly crisscrossing in odd places. The people toys (pages 44, 46, and 48) are designed with minimal seaming—especially on their faces.

Most toy seams appear along the mid line, something our eyes have learned to accept in our clothing. A good way to hide a seam is along a color change. A seam is necessary here anyway, so it can be used to create shape as well as change color. The Duck (page 42) serves as the best example of seams hidden by color changes—an intriguing puzzle to assemble. Most toy seams can be sewn from the reverse side for less obvious seams, although you may need to add seam allowances to maintain the proper shape. These stitches will show when the toy is firmly stuffed and the seam opens a bit.

Darts are partial seams used to give shape. This means two pattern pieces have been blended together with only part of the seam left—the dart. The Duck's head pattern has two darts, one for the bill and the other for the top of the head. When sewing darts, be sure to taper the end of the dart as marked to achieve a smooth shape.

To avoid re-threading when hand-sewing toys with changes of fabric color or type, use a needle for each color of thread needed. Tuck the extra threaded needle (a short "sharp" quilting needle is best) into the fabric to avoid tangles and pricks. Machine sewing may require several changes of thread color—which is a pain—so consider using colorless monofilament thread.

Cutting out these tiny toys requires accuracy, but you can correct a little on seam length by pinning the ends of the matching pieces together and easing the longer side to the shorter.

Malcolm, the Duck

This pattern makes a 3" duck. For a female mallard, use all tan felt and brown embroidery trim.

Materials

Back: 3" x 3" tan felt
Head: 1-1/2" x 3" green felt
Belly, Thigh, and Neck Band: 3" x 5" white felt
Tail and Chest: 1-3/4" x 2" black felt
Feet: 2" x 3" yellow felt
Feet Liners: 1" x 2" stiff plastic*
White (W), yellow (Y), green (G), black (B), and tan (T) thread
Eyes: Two 1/8" black beads
Fiberfill stuffing
Scissors, needles, stuffing tool

A butter tub lid works well

▲ *When it rains a duck will quack.*
As water runs right off his back.

1. Pattern: Cut out all pattern pieces.
2. Align the Back pieces, tuck in folded Tail, and sew (T).
3. Match and sew the Belly top edge to the Back lower edge (T). Repeat.

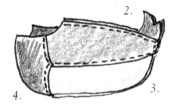

4. Align the Chest to the Back/Belly front edge and sew (B). Repeat for the other side.
5. Join Neck Band to the Chest top edge and sew (T).

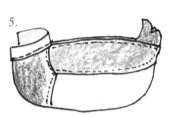

6. Align the Head and Neck Band top edge and sew (G).

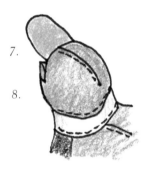

7. Sew the Head top and Chin seams.
8. Center the Upper Bill to the Head seam and sew (G).

Center the Lower Bill to the Head Neck and sew.

9. Sew Head darts (G). Align the Bills and sew (Y). Stuff the Bill firmly.

10. Sew Neck Band front (W). Sew Chest seams (B). Sew Belly seams to C (W), leaving thread attached.

11. Stuff the duck firmly, beginning with the Head.

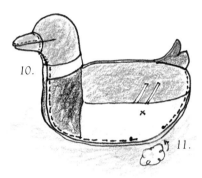

12. Whip-stitch C to D closed.

13. Sew on two black Eyes. Sew (W) angled wing markings on each Back side.

14. Legs: Sew the button to the inside Thigh (see Button Joints, page 26).
A. Sew Thigh to the Leg (Y).
B. Insert Foot Liner: Match the Foot Top to Leg Foot and sew (Y); continue up Leg.

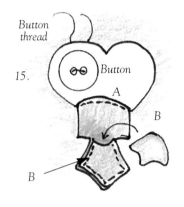

C. Align Thigh edges and sew (W) part way, stuff the Leg firmly, and sew closed. Repeat.

15. Joint: (See Button Joints, page 26.) Use a strong double thread, knot it, sew through the inside of the Leg and back, through the body, through the opposite leg and back, through the Body, and sew a double knot.

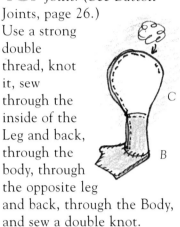

Duck Pattern

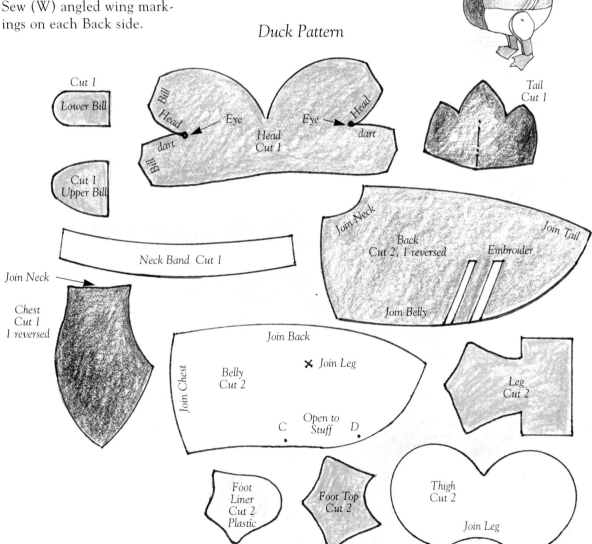

Cut 1
Lower Bill

Cut 1
Upper Bill

Bill
Head
Bill
dart

Eye

Head
Cut 1

Eye
Head
dart

Tail
Cut 1

Neck Band Cut 1

Join Neck

Chest
Cut 1
1 reversed

Join Chest

Join Neck

Back
Cut 2, 1 reversed

Join Tail

Embroider

Join Belly

Join Back

Belly
Cut 2

✗ Join Leg

C   Open to
Stuff   D

Leg
Cut 2

Foot
Liner
Cut 2
Plastic

Foot Top
Cut 2

Thigh
Cut 2

Join Leg

12 # Tom, the Boy

*This pattern makes a 3-1/4" tall boy. All
kinds of variations are possible: change his
hair color, change his outfit to baseball, or
make him all flesh-colored and sew tiny
clothes to fit. Note: Use thread colors
indicated if sewing by hand. For a sewing
machine, use monofilament colorless
thread. Sew from the reverse side where
possible.*

▲ *Tiny Tom moves his small arms.
He hopes you'll fall for his small charms.*

Materials

Head and Hands: 1-1/2" x 6" flesh felt
Arms and Shirt: 2" x 4-1/2" light blue felt
Legs and Pants: 2" x 4-1/4"dark blue felt
Hair and Shoe Soles: 2-1/4" x 2-1/2" black felt
Fiberfill stuffing
Blue (LB and DB), white (W), brown (Br), and flesh
 (F) thread

Black, bright pink, bright blue, and white embroidery
 floss
Eyes: Two 1/8" black beads
Buttons: Four small white beads
Embroidery needle, sharp scissors, needles, stuffing
 tool, needle for each thread color (optional)

1. Pattern: Cut out all
pattern pieces.
2. Body:
A. Fold Head and sew Chin
and Forehead seams. Align
the Head dart and sew (F).
B. Align Chest pieces and sew
front seam (LB).
C. Align Pants pieces and sew
the front (DB).
D. Open Head, Chest, and
Pants pieces. Match seams and
sew Head to Chest and Chest
to Body (LB).
E. Align the Body edges and
sew the back seam from top to
bottom.

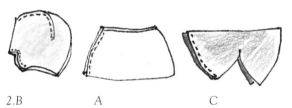

2.B   A   C

3. Stuff: First stuff the Chin
and Nose to shape and then
fill the toy firmly. Align the
Pants seam and whip-stitch
closed.

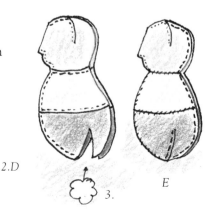

2.D   3.   E

44 *Tiny Toys*

4. Face:

A. Use the bright pink embroidery floss (two or three strands) to sew the Mouth. Knot ends under collar to hide them.

B. Change to black floss and sew the Eye beads.

C. Sew the Hair seam from the wrong side (Br). Match Hair seams with Head seams, mold the Hair.

D. Whip-stitch the collar on (W) and sew bead buttons on the shirt front.

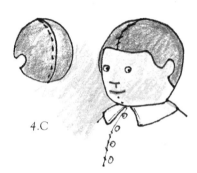

4.C

5. Arm: Sew the Hand to the Sleeve. Repeat. Fold the Arm and sew a 1/8" stitch to form the Thumb (F). Sew the Hand (F). Sew the sleeve (LB) to 1/2" from the end of the seam, stuff the Arm firmly, and whip-stitch closed. Repeat.

Stitch Thumb

5.

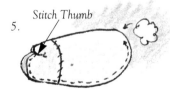

6. Leg: Sew the Foot to the Leg (DB). Sew (DB) up the entire leg seam. Sew (W or white embroidery floss) Shoe front. Stuff the Leg firmly and align the Foot. Whip-stitch or

button hole stitch the Foot in place. At the top of the Shoe seam, sew a bow knot. Sew running shoe lines (DB). Repeat.

6.

Boy Pattern

7. Finish: Join the Arms and Legs (see Sewn Joints, page 16 or 27). Use a strong double thread knotted to sew through one Leg, through the Body, and through the other Leg. Pull tight and knot. Join the Arms in the same manner. Clip the thread.

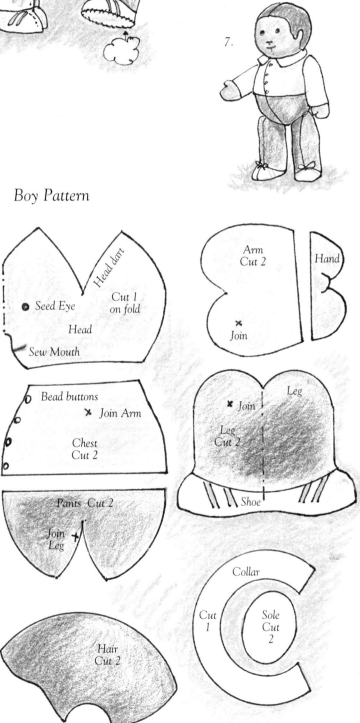

7.

13 Blast Off, the Astronaut

This pattern makes a 4" tall astronaut. His helmet is removable and can be tried on several of the other toys for size.

▲ This astronaut stares at the stars.
He hopes one day to walk on Mars.

Materials

Head and Hands: 1-1/2" x 6" flesh felt
Body and Helmet: 4-1/2" x 9" silver-faced fabric
Hair: 2" x 5" tan felt
Shoes: 3" x 4" metallic gold fabric
Soles: 2-1/4" x 2-1/2" black felt
Belt: 12" of silver Mylar ribbon
Eyes: Two 1/8" black beads
Fiberfill stuffing

Blues (LB and DB), white (W), brown (Br), and flesh (F) threads
Black, bright pink, bright blue, and white embroidery floss
Embroidery needle, sharp scissors, needles, stuffing tool, needle for each thread (optional)
Note: Sew fabric seams from the reverse side.

1. Make the Astronaut the same as the Boy (page 44) except for these changes:
2. Body: Sew Head to Body. Sew seams, stuff, and close. Tie silver ribbons around neck and waist.

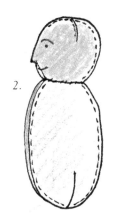

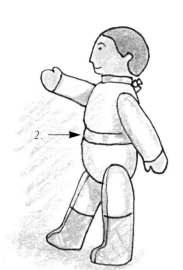

3. Helmet: Align and top-stitch the window of clear plastic on the inside of the flat Helmet piece over the Face hole. Sew the Helmet back seam, back-stitching at the bottom edge. Sew the Helmet darts across the top. Turn right side out.

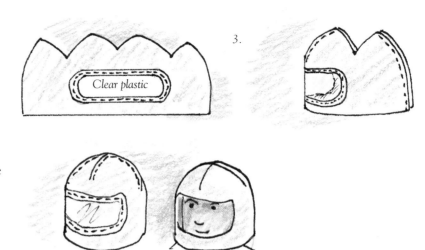

Astronaut Pattern

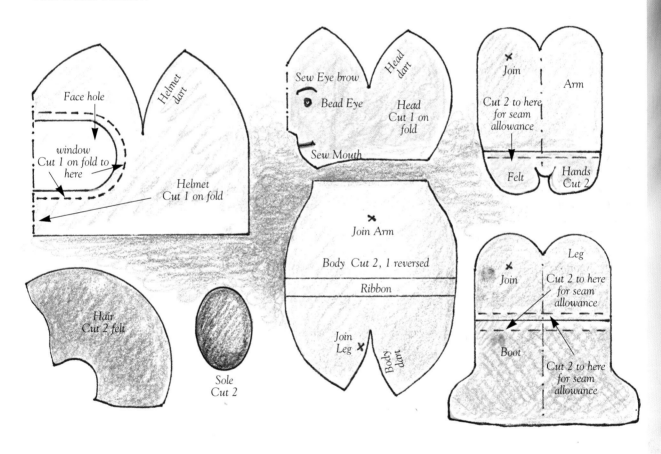

Face hole

window
Cut 1 on fold to here

Helmet
dart

Helmet
Cut 1 on fold

Hair
Cut 2 felt

Sole
Cut 2

Sew Eye brow

Bead Eye

Head
dart

Head
Cut 1 on fold

Sew Mouth

Join Arm

Body Cut 2, 1 reversed

Ribbon

Join
Leg

Body
dart

Join

Cut 2 to here
for seam
allowance

Arm

Felt

Hands
Cut 2

Join

Leg

Cut 2 to here
for seam
allowance

Boot

Cut 2 to here
for seam
allowance

Have You Thought of This?

Arrange a collection of small toys on a wreath, tie them on with cord or wire, and add a ribbon. Basic straw and grapevine wreaths are available in craft stores along with wire and ribbons.

14

Angelica, the Angel

This pattern makes a 4" tall angel. The people dolls (pages 44, 46, and the two shown here) can make up a family for a doll house. For the girl at right, vary the Boy pattern (page 44), use the Angel's hair, and add a circle skirt.

▲ *Angels visit when there's need*
To help us out with one good deed.

Materials

Head, Arms, Legs: 4" x 6" flesh felt
Body: 3" x 4" silver knit fabric
Hair: 2" x 5" tan felt
Petticoat: 3" x 8" lightweight white fabric
Lace trim: 8" of 1/8" elastic
Dress: 4" x 20" netting
Belt: 24" of 1/8" wide coral ribbon
Wings: Metallic gold pipe cleaner or 3" x 6" gold fabric

Fiberfill stuffing
Matching threads
Black and bright pink embroidery thread
Eyes: Two 1/8" blue beads
Sharp scissors, needles, stuffing tool, embroidery needle, needle for each thread (optional)

Note: Sew most seams from the reverse side.

1. Make the Angel the same as the Boy (page 44) except for these changes:
2. Hair: Seam Hair and darts. Join the Hair like the Boy.
3. Clothing:
A. Petticoat: Sew the lace trim to the petticoat bottom edge. Match the side seams and sew to the top edge. Run a gathering thread across the top and pull to match the Body diameter. Sew on narrow elastic and slide onto the doll.

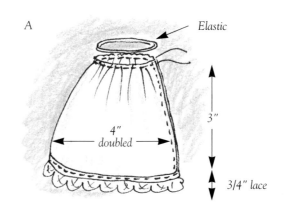

A

Elastic

3"

4" doubled

3/4" lace

B. Dress: Measure 5" from the dress side and cut an Arm hole 1/2" long. Repeat for the other side. Run a gathering thread across the top of the dress. Pull the thread and gather to 3". Sew over the gathering threads to secure. Put the dress on the angel with the opening in the back.

C. Ribbon: Wrap the ribbon around the Angel's Waist and cross the ends in the back over the Shoulders. Cross again over the Chest and around to the Back. Tie a bow.

D. Wings: Twist the pipe cleaner to the shape shown and wrap the end around the Neck to hold Wings in place.

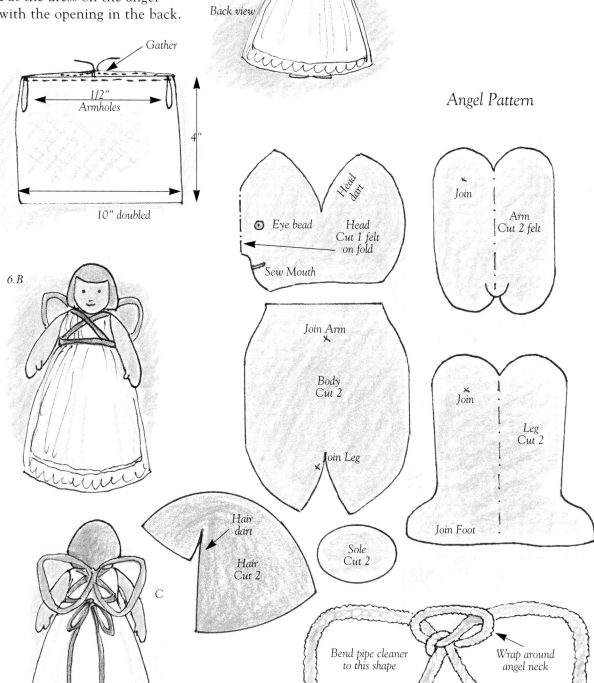

Gather

1/2"
Armholes

4"

10" doubled

Back view

Angel Pattern

6.B

Head
dart

Eye bead

Head
Cut 1 felt
on fold

Sew Mouth

Join

Arm
Cut 2 felt

Join Arm

Body
Cut 2

Join Leg

Join

Leg
Cut 2

Join Foot

Hair
dart

Hair
Cut 2

Sole
Cut 2

C

Bend pipe cleaner
to this shape

Wrap around
angel neck

15

Safari, the Lion

This pattern makes a 4" long lion (plus tail).

➤ *The lion joins a lion pride Looking for a lion bride.*

Materials

Head, Body, and Legs: 4-1/2" x 10" tan felt
Mane and Ruff: 2-1/2" x 6" brown felt
Chin: 1/2" x 1" white felt
Eyes: Two 1/8" black beads
Tail: 6" brown yarn

Fiberfill stuffing
Matching tan threads
Black embroidery floss
Sharp scissors, needle, stuffing tool

1. Pattern: Cut out all pattern pieces.
2. Chin: Match Chin top to Nose mark on Face and sew with tan thread.

3. Face: Align the Face to the Ruff and sew from the reverse side.
4. Mane: Fold Mane piece and sew the top dart with brown thread. Match Mane to Ruff and sew. Join the Mane to the Body and sew.

Have You Thought of This?
Robert Hueter may wear a Detroit Lion football team mascot on his hat, but he says he prefers the Tampa team.

5. Tail: Make three 1" loops of brown yarn. Sew the loop ends to the Tail end. Fold Tail lengthwise over loops and sew across tail end. Clip Tuft ends evenly. Sew Tail side seam. Angle the Tail downward on the Body and sew the end into the Body seam.

6. Body: Fold the Body to match. Sew from the Body back across the Tail end to D. Sew from the Chin to C.

7. Stuff: Fill the Lion with fiberfill and sew C to D closed.

8. Place Ears on Mane and whip-stitch them on. With black embroidery floss, sew the Lion's face as shown. Sew whisker dots and Eye marks. Sew black Eye beads on.

9. Legs: (See page 26 for Button Joints or page 27 for Sewn Joints.) Fold the Leg and sew from top to Foot, stuff firmly and sew closed. Repeat. Use a strong double thread knotted to sew through one leg, through the body, and through the other leg. Pull tight and knot. Clip the thread.

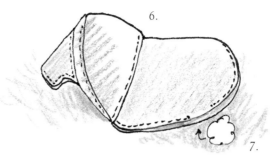

6.

7.

8.
Ears

5.

Lion Pattern

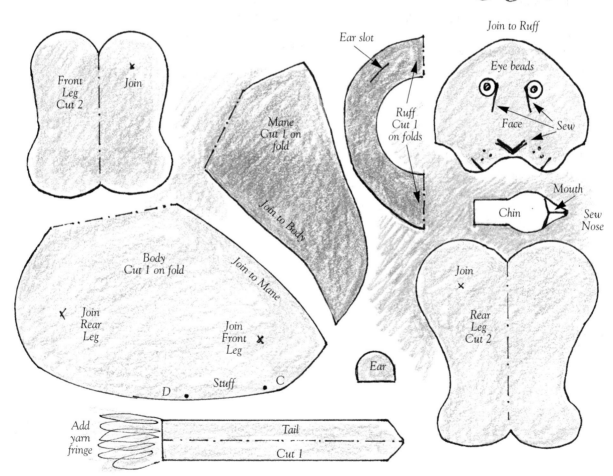

Front Leg Cut 2

Join

Mane Cut 1 on fold

Join to Body

Join to Mane

Ear slot

Ruff Cut 1 on folds

Join to Ruff

Eye beads

Face

Sew

Mouth

Chin

Sew Nose

Join

Rear Leg Cut 2

Body Cut 1 on fold

Join Rear Leg

Join Front Leg

Stuff

D

C

Ear

Add yarn fringe

Tail Cut 1

Surface Decoration and Fabrics

Chapter 4

Fabrics for Toys

Fabrics for Tiny Toys have special requirements because of their small sizes, narrow seam allowances, and the stress of turning and stuffing. This limits the fabrics you can use. The prime consideration is the appearance—the color and texture you want. For ease of sewing and wearability you want a non-fraying, firmly woven, or double-knit fabric for strong seams and narrow seam allowances. Fabrics should be flexible for molding to shape, color-fast in case kids chew on them, and washable for clean toys.

Look for fabrics with as many of these qualities as possible. You won't find all of them in one fabric. I found a great black and white cow-print cotton flannel fabric and tried to sew the cow pattern. Alas, the fabric was too softly woven and pulled out on the seams. What to do? A collection of cut-out felt spots appliquéd on a white felt cow looked fine.

Use the best fabric you can; you won't need much. These fabrics are used in this book: felt, berber cloth, polyester knit with overlay print, fleece, faux fur, metallic lame, lace, net, knit suede cloth, plastic foam sheet, imitation leather, ribbons, and small bits of others.

Some fabrics may be difficult to use: velvet frays and sheds nap, cotton or wool flannels fray and the weave is too loose, most fur fabric is not flexible enough and long fur fibers blur shape, cotton broadcloth has an unimaginative surface and may not flex enough, leather is probably too thick or not strong enough to hold seams, and shantung is probably too stiff to mold to shape.

The more experience you gain in making Tiny Toys, the more you'll be able to experiment with unusual fabrics. When bits and pieces of fabric are scavenged from your stash, you can't always identify them. Try cutting and sewing a fabric. If it frays, abrades, stretches too much, pulls out, or makes some other kind of mess, give up and use felt or a better fabric.

◄ Fabrics (upper left to right clockwise): decorative lightweight metallic polyester knit, gold dots on black, animal print lightweight velour, silver metallic and peach knit fabric, (center) golden tan heavier weight velour stretch knit, metallic design stamped on black knit polyester, gray 3/8" faux fur polyester, (below) tan 1/2" faux fur polyester, (lower right) creamy white 1/4" faux fur, (going left) two tweed craft felt squares and three colors of craft felt.

Sewing Decorative Fabrics

Decorative fabrics may be soft and shifting and thus need stabilizing for machine sewing. For this, do not cut out the fabric pieces. Instead, trace the pattern on paper. Lay the paper pattern on the fabric folded double (face side in). Pin in place and sew the seam lines with very short stitches. Remove the paper and trim away the extra fabric, leaving a 1/8" seam allowance. Some pieces, such as feet bottoms and head tops, will be too small to machine sew and must be finished by hand.

To hand-sew flimsy fabrics, sew them from the wrong side with a tiny whip-stitch. From the right side, such as closing seams, tuck the seam allowance in with your needle and sew hidden stitches.

Embellishing Fabrics

Sometimes you can find just the perfect fabric or felt for a toy. Happy day! But sometimes perfect-looking fabric frays, or the nap is too long, or it doesn't come in the right color or the right size spots, or you want a specific design. You can embellish the surface with embroidery done by hand or sewing machine, or by painting or printing it.

Embroidery

Hand embroidery can be done on fabric pieces before they are cut out or after the toys are sewn and stuffed. You may prefer to sew on a toy that is stuffed but not assembled. Use cotton embroidery floss which comes in a wide range of colors, or rayon embroidery thread which has more sheen, or use sewing machine thread doubled or quadrupled if that's what you have on hand.

Fabric must be machine embroidered before the pattern is cut out. Maneuvering tiny fabric pieces in the sewing machine is next to impossible. Use tailor's chalk to trace pattern pieces on fabric as shown and use a stabilizing paper on the back to prevent puckering. Group the pieces so the pattern can be sewn continuously. The stitching will contract the fabric. When all machine-sewn decorative stitching is completed, retrace the pattern pieces and cut them out. Add a touch of FrayChek to stop threads from raveling. Continue making the toy according to the instructions. (For examples of machine-embroidered Tiny Toys, see the Kitty and Tiger, pages 56 and 58, respectively.)

Painting

Suppose you want more shading than you can find in available fabric or achieve by embroidery. You can use paint to brush or print your designs on fabric. Artist's acrylic paints, which come in tubes or jars, are water-soluble but dry waterproof. Mix the colors you want and lightly brush the color on the fabric with a stiff bristle brush. Apply the color carefully because splotches are hard to remove. Little fibers stick up on felt and other fabrics so you'll need to brush the color in. Aim for a dry-brush style noted on the Kangaroo (page 63). Thick paint will change the texture of the fabric. Practice first on a piece of matching felt. To stipple, lightly dab straight down with the brush for a dot pattern. For a dry brush, angle the brush and stroke to lay paint on the surface. Some artists make toys of percale, a flat, tightly-woven fabric, and then paint solidly like an artist's canvas. Wash brushes in soap and water immediately after use.

Printing

Designs can be printed on fabrics. To do this, fashion a printing block by carving the end of a stick, a carrot stick, or piece of potato, mix the color of acrylic paint wanted, dip the printer in the paint, and press it onto the toy. The Giraffe (page 66) is done this way.

Print the design on fabric before making the toy, after the toy is stuffed but not assembled, or when the toy is finished. A word of caution: If you've spent a lot of time and effort making a toy, test your printer, paint color, and paint on spare fabric before going at a finished toy.

16

Wrecks, the Tyrannosaurus

The giant Tyrannosaurus Rex shrinks to a manageable 6-1/2" size. Other dinosaurs, sewn in decorative fabrics, the author designed are shown on the next page. To design your own toys, see Chapter 8.

▲ *Tyrannosaurus Rex is gone. Big stone footprints linger on.*

Materials

Body: 4" x 9" green felt (or desired color)
Eyes: Two beads (gold, gray, yellow or desired color)
Green and white thread, strong thread for joints

Polyester stuffing
Scissors, needle, stuffing tool

1. Pattern: Trace all pattern pieces on felt, or pin the pattern on fabric and cut out.

2. Front Legs: Fold double and whip-stitch or machine top-stitch to reinforce the felt.

3. Body: Match the Body pieces and sew from the Nose A down the Neck to C, the opening to stuff. Knot the thread. Sew from the Head B to D.

4. Head: Match the Head center with the Nose seam. Align the Head sides with the Head top and sew. (See Step 11.)

5. Stuff: Fill the Head first with stuffing to sculpture the shape as you fill it. When the Body is packed full, sew the seam closed.

6. Legs: Match two Leg pieces and sew from the heel around the top to the toe and stuff. Repeat.

7. Feet: Align the Foot with the Leg and whip-stitch halfway. Stuff the Foot firmly and sew closed. Repeat.

8. Joints: See page 26 for Button Joints or page 27 for Sewn Joints.

9. Front Legs: Whip-stitch the front Legs to the Body.

10. Eyes: Sew on Eye beads.

11. Mouth: Machine zigzag the Mouth before joining Body pieces or hand-sew a zigzag mouth.

6.

7.

5.

2. Front Legs
9. Join to Body

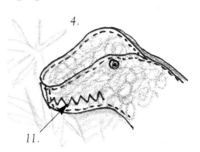

4.

11.

Tyrannosaurus Rex Pattern

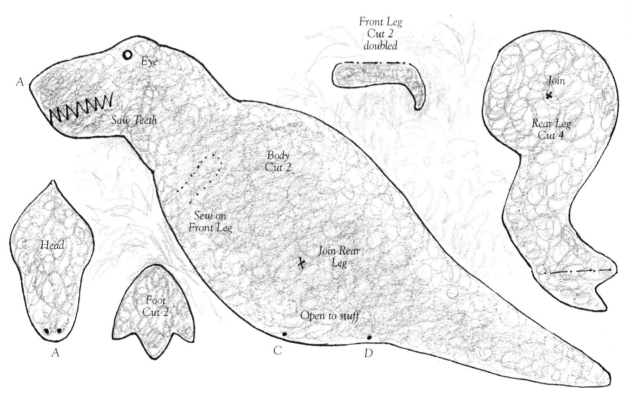

Front Leg
Cut 2
doubled

Join

Rear Leg
Cut 4

A

Eye

Saw Teeth

Body
Cut 2

Sew on
Front Leg

Head

Join Rear
Leg

Foot
Cut 2

Open to stuff

A

C

D

Have You Thought of This?

Here's a dinosaur birthday cake to delight a child's eyes, and chocolate cake inside to delight his or her tummy. Use foil or clear wrap to keep the frosting off of the toys. (Tree and volcano by Hattie Stroud.)

17

Jessie, the Kitty

This pattern makes a 3-1/2" long cat (plus tail). The next three patterns show how to machine-embroider toys before cutting out the pattern. For a Siamese cat, use this pattern with the changes shown at right.

▲ Cats who are too very curious
Get into things that are injurious.

Materials

Head, Body, Tail, and Legs: 6" x 9" gold felt
Paws, Muzzle, Tail Tip: 2" x 9" white felt
Eye color: 1/2" x 1/2" bright green felt
Fiberfill stuffing
Matching gold (G) and white (W) threads

Brown embroidery floss
Bright orange machine embroidery thread
Eyes: Two 1/8" black beads
Needle, stuffing tool, sharp scissors

Surface decoration: To hand embroider, apply hand embroidery designs when the cat is completed but before the Legs and Tail are joined.

To machine embroider:

1. Embroider the cat before cutting out the pattern. To do this, align the 6" x 9" gold felt to the 2" x 9" white felt, with the gold overlapping 1/8" and baste the seam. Trace the pattern on this as laid out with the Feet on white, Body on gold. Use removable tailor's chalk because the stitching may contract the felt, and new lines may be needed.

Note doubled pattern in reverse

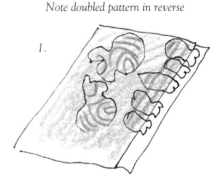

1.

Have You Thought of This?

Special treats for the ones you love on Valentine's Day can include such delights as a stuffed Siamese cat you've made, a box of candy, an affectionate greeting card, and a potted plant.

2. Set your machine to a pattern stitch (zigzag, feather-stitch, or similar design). Use the stitching guide given to sew across the Legs and Tail in horizontal stripes and then sew the Body. Make the bottom stitching row exactly at the joining between white and gold to secure the joining. Remove basting stitches if they show.

3. When all machine-sewn decorative stitching is completed, retrace the pattern pieces. Cut out pattern pieces and dab FrayChek on loose threads.

4. Sew the Kitty similar to the Tiny Teddy (page 14), except with these changes:
A. Sew the Belly to one Body side, from B to E, and proceed as given.

B. Sew the Muzzle dart, then sew it on the completed and stuffed Head.
C. Sew the green felt Eye piece on and sew on the black Eye bead. Repeat.

4.

Kitty Pattern

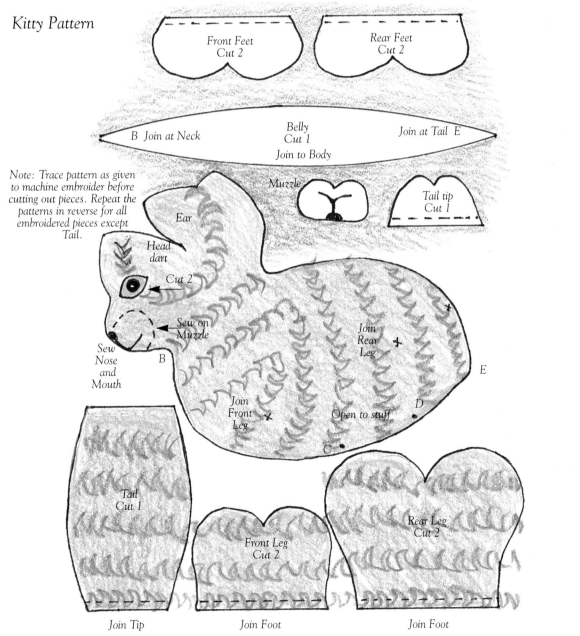

Front Feet
Cut 2

Rear Feet
Cut 2

B Join at Neck — Belly Cut 1 — Join at Tail E

Join to Body

Note: Trace pattern as given to machine embroider before cutting out pieces. Repeat the patterns in reverse for all embroidered pieces except Tail.

Muzzle

Tail tip
Cut 1

Ear

Head dart

Cut 2

Sew on Muzzle

Sew Nose and Mouth

B

Join Rear Leg

E

D

Open to stuff

Join Front Leg

C

Tail
Cut 1

Front Leg
Cut 2

Rear Leg
Cut 2

Join Tip

Join Foot

Join Foot

18

Flame, the Tiger

This pattern makes a 4" long tiger (plus tail).

▲ *The tiger has such beautiful hair*
She wears her fur coat everywhere.

Materials

Head, Body, and Legs: 6" x 10" orange felt
Legs, Muzzle, and Tail: 2" x 9" white felt
Eyes: Two 1/8" green beads
Fiberfill stuffing

Matching threads
Black embroidery floss
Stuffing tool

1. Pattern and surface deco-ration: Proceed the same as the Kitty to hand or machine embroidery the pieces. Join felt colors, lay out the pattern doubled in reverse as shown, machine embroider the designs and cut out the pieces.
2. Sew the Tiger similar to the Tiny Teddy (page 14) and the Kitty (page 56), except with these changes:
A. Machine embroider black Ears on orange, then cut them out or appliqué black Ear patches on Ears.
B. Sew the Belly to one Body side, from B to E, and proceed as given.
C. Satin-stitch with black along the spine and on the Tail tip.
D. Face: Sew the Muzzle dart, then sew it on the completed and stuffed Head.
E. Embroider the black Eye triangle and sew on the green Eye bead. Repeat.
F. Hand satin-stitch the Nose with orange embroidery floss.

Tiger Pattern

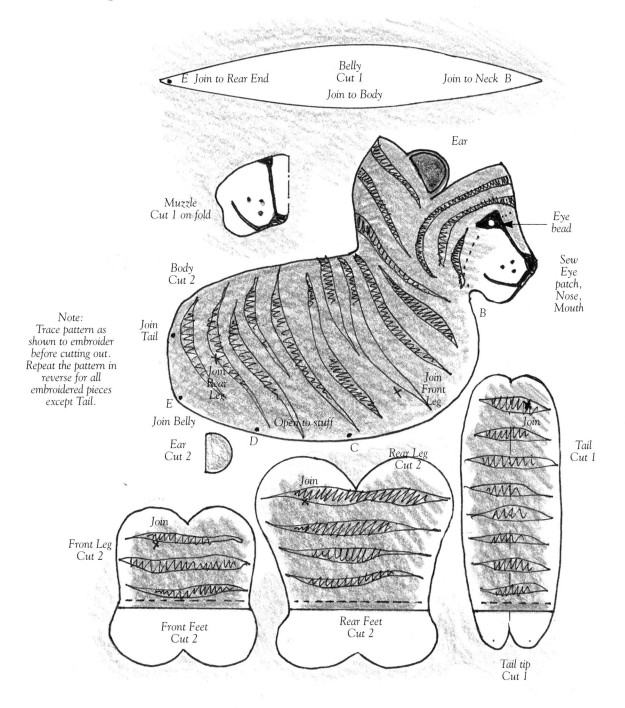

E Join to Rear End

Belly
Cut 1

Join to Neck B

Join to Body

Ear

Muzzle
Cut 1 on fold

Eye
bead

Sew
Eye
patch,
Nose,
Mouth

Body
Cut 2

Join
Tail

Note:
Trace pattern as
shown to embroider
before cutting out.
Repeat the pattern in
reverse for all
embroidered pieces
except Tail.

Join
Rear
Leg

B

Join
Front
Leg

Join

Tail
Cut 1

E

Join Belly

Open to stuff

Ear
Cut 2

D

C

Rear Leg
Cut 2

Join

Front Leg
Cut 2

Join

Join

Front Feet
Cut 2

Rear Feet
Cut 2

Tail tip
Cut 1

19

Sheldon, the Sea Turtle

This pattern makes a 7" turtle, including the tail. The pattern is machine-embroidered on the shell before sewing the turtle.

▲ *Sea turtles crawl up on the land*
To lay their eggs deep in the sand.

Materials

Shells: 5" x 8" dark green felt
Head: 2-1/2" x 4" print fabric
Flippers: 3" x 6" pea green felt or print fabric
Eyes: 3mm black beads
Matching thread, tan machine embroidery thread
Fiberfill stuffing and pellets
Sewing machine, sharp scissors, stuffing tool

Surface decoration: Apply machine embroidery when the shell darts are seamed before proceeding any further. Apply hand embroidery when the turtle is stuffed.

1. Pattern: Trace pattern on felt and cut out. Add seam allowances for fabric.
2. Shell top: Sew the Shell darts on the wrong side. Set the machine to a narrow zigzag and embroider the design shown. Satin stitch around the Shell. Fold the

Tail and satin stitch the edge closed. Stuff with fiberfill.

2.

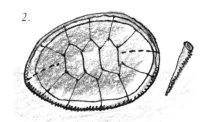

Have You Thought of This?

For sea dwellers that appear to swim through the air, tie an assortment of them on dowel rods to make a mobile. The secret is to balance each rod from the bottom upward. Make adjustments by sliding the center string on the dowel to find the center of gravity.

3. Head: Sew the Head top to the Shell top. Sew the Head bottom to the Shell bottom. Align and seam the Head and turn. Stuff the Head with fiberfill.

4. Flippers: Match a pair of front Flippers, seam, and stuff with pellets. Repeat for all Legs.

5. Shells: Align the Flippers and Tail to the top Shell and pin. Sew the Shells together with C to D open to stuff. Pour in pellets. Sew closed.

6. Sew on black Eye beads.

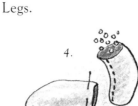

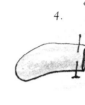

Sea Turtle Pattern

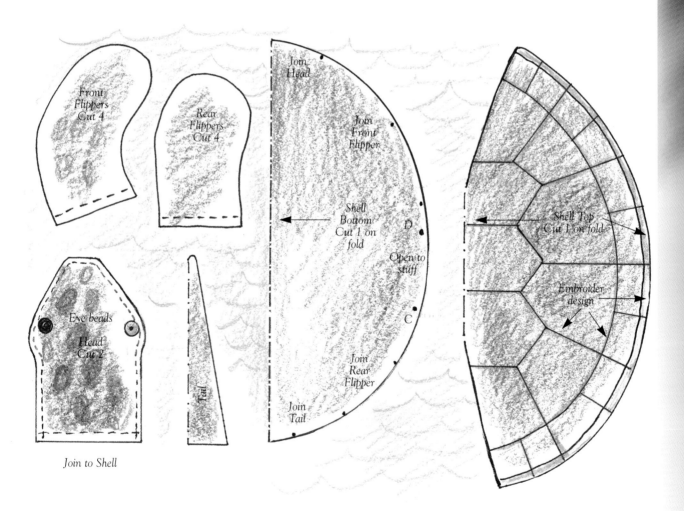

20

Boing, the Kangaroo

This 6-1/2" kangaroo can be painted to achieve shading.

▲ *Hippity hop goes kangaroo.*
She can jump much farther than you.

Materials

Body: 4" x 9" tan, gold, or peach felt
Eyes: Two black beads
Matching thread, black thread, strong thread
   for joints
Polyester stuffing
Sewing machine, stuffing tool

1. Pattern: Trace the pattern and cut out.

2. Front Legs: Fold lengthwise and machine top-stitch or whip-stitch. Stuff firmly and hand-sew closed. Repeat.

3. Body: Match Body and sew from the Nose to the Ear slot. Sew from the opposite Ear slot around the Tail to D.

4. Head: On the reverse side, match the Ear slot edges. Fold and tuck the folded Ears into the Ear slot and sew Ears upward. Turn right side out. Sew from the Nose to D.

5. Stuff: Stuff the Nose first with fiberfill and pack the Body full. Sew the Body closed from C to D.

6. Pouch: For a female kangaroo, align the Pouch over the front seam and hand sew in place.

7. Legs:
A. Back Legs. Sew in button. Match Leg pieces and sew from D to Toe. Sew from C to the Toe. Fold the Foot, match seams, and sew across the Toes. Stuff the Leg and Foot firmly and sew C to D closed. Repeat.
B. Front Legs: Fold and sew. Stuff and sew closed. Repeat.
C. Join Legs as described: Use button joints (page 26) for the back Legs. Make hand-sewn joints (page 27) for the front Legs.

4.

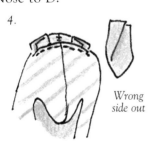

Wrong side out

5.

6.

7A.

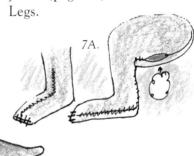

8. Face: Sew small black Eye beads in place.

9. Color: (To paint, see Painting, page 53.)
A. Use artist's acrylic paints, a stiff bristle artist's brush, white pan or pallet, and jar of water.
B. Put ocher, sienna, white, and black on the white pan.

Mix the color you want and dilute with water to achieve a creamy consistency. In the "dry brush" technique, color is laid on rather than penetrating the fibers. Practice on a piece of matching felt. For dry brush, angle the brush and stroke to lay paint on the surface.

C. Paint the Sides, Face, and Back with a mix of ocher, sienna, and a dab of white. To shade darker, eliminate the white and paint over the Back color.

D. Paint Nose, Toes, and Ear edges black.

E. If you make a mistake, wait until the color dries and pick the paint off the fibers it is sitting on. (It sounds weird, but it works!) Blend in the proper color over the removed fibers and let it dry.

Kangaroo Pattern

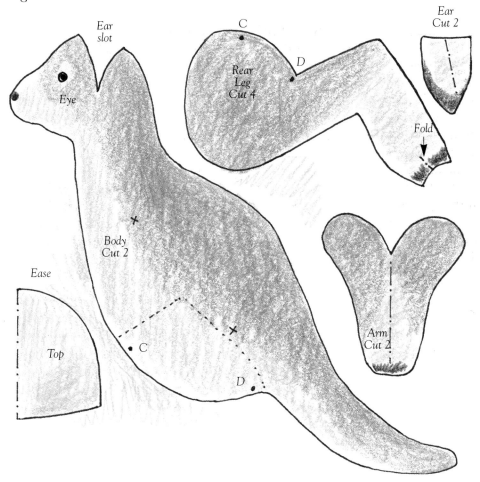

*A*rmatures

Many Tiny Toys can stand up by themselves. The outer fabric and firmly packed inner stuffing can keep a tiny leg stiff. Toys with long necks, legs, or wings may need more support. For small toys, bamboo skewers from the grocery store are ideal; they're lightweight, inexpensive, and easy to cut. For the Giraffe and Moose legs (pages 67 and 69, respectively), skewers were wrapped in fiberfill, pushed into the partly stuffed leg and clipped off to length. When the foot is sewn closed, no armature shows but it keeps the piece stiff.

To make moveable arms, legs, or tails stiffer, you can use pipe cleaners called chenille stems which come with long fibers in a variety colors. They can be inserted into the toy for support and flexibility or left exposed for feet or horns. The Bat's (page 74) brown pipe cleaners are couched by zigzag sewing machine stitching onto the wings. A curled brown pipe cleaner makes the Monkey's (page 70) tail.

Making Surface Design Choices

How do you get spots on a toy giraffe? You may be lucky enough to find a small giraffe print in a fabric store. If not, make your own animal print in one of several ways. You can apply the design several ways: before you cut out the pattern, after sewing the toy parts before they are assembled, or after the toy is finished.

1. Cut out brown five-sided spots and appliqué them on the toy.

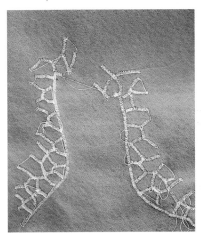

2. Choose gold or rust felt and machine satin-stitch the spaces between the spots. Or hand-embroider brown spots on cream felt.

3. Use artist's acrylic paint and a small stiff bristle artist's brush to paint on spots.

4. Block print the spots on with a potato dipped in paint.

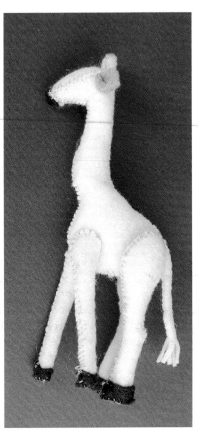

First make the toy in a plain felt or fabric. You can apply the spots before assembling the legs or after.

Carve a potato or carrot into printers for large and small spots. Dip the printer into paint the right consistency to print.

Practice printing on scrap fabric. When all works well, carefully press paint spots on the Giraffe. If you mess up, wait until it dries and pick off the paint.

The photo provides a guide for the pattern of spots to print on this elegant animal.

Stretch, the Giraffe

21

This makes a 6" tall giraffe. The model for this toy peers over the wall from her home at the Detroit Zoo.

▶ *For a realistic looking toy, use a stiff brush to apply paint or print designs on the toy. Use a picture of the animal as a guide.*

▲ *Her head gets lost up in a cloud.
Her view is perfect in a crowd.*

Materials

Body: 6" x 9" flesh or light tan felt
Hooves: 1-1/2" x 2" brown felt or foam sheet*
Eyes: Two black beads
Armatures: Bamboo skewers or stove pipe wire
Matching thread, black thread for Mouth, strong
   thread for joints
Polyester stuffing

Paint: Artist's acrylic brown and sienna paint, stiff
   brush, carved printer (a potato or carrot will do)
   or brown felt for appliqué spots 3" x 3"
Buttons for joints: Two 1/2" and two 7/16" buttons
Scissors, two needles, stuffing tool
Darice Foamies were used in this project

Spots: See the previous page for block printing spots before or after sewing the toy.

1. Pattern: Trace all pattern pieces on felt and cut out.

2. Body: Match Body pieces and sew from the Nose down to C. Sew from the top of the Neck to D.

3.
Head: A. Fold the Ear twice as shown, tuck it into the Ear slot with folds forward, and pin or stitch to hold. Fold the slot over the Ear and sew it closed. Repeat.

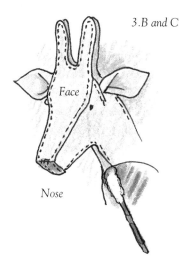
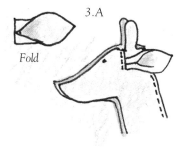

B. Sew the Nose to the Face. C. Match the Nose tip with the Nose seam, match the Horns, and whip-stitch.

4. Stuff: Stuff the Head partly full. Push the blunt end of a skewer up the Neck into the Horn and break the skewer off at 3". Repeat. Continue to push stuffing into the Body and around the Neck skewers until it is packed full. Sew the Body closed.

5. Legs:

A. Overlap the Hoof 1/4" on the Leg and hand sew or satin-stitch to join.

B. Leg button joints (see page 26): Sew a strong thread through the inside of the Leg, through a button, and back, leaving 6" long thread uncut.

C. Fold the Leg lengthwise and sew from fold top to Hoof. Knot but don't cut the thread.

D. Leg Armatures: Push a wad of stuffing into the top of the Leg in front of the button with room left for the armature. To wrap a skewer in fiberfill, hold a loose wad of fibers, dampen the skewer tip, and twist the skewer in the fiberfill to wrap tightly for 3". Push the wrapped rod into the Leg to 1/4" from the top. Rewrap to add stuffing if needed. Break off the skewer at the Hoof and trim. Sew the Hoof closed. Repeat A to D for all Legs.

E. Joining the Legs: Rethread the dangling Leg button thread and sew through the Body, Hoofs frontward, and leave threads hanging. Sew the opposite Leg button thread through Body. Pull the Leg thread firmly to seat one Leg and tie a triple knot around the opposite button Leg

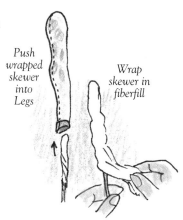

Push wrapped skewer into Legs

Wrap skewer in fiberfill

thread. Repeat for the opposite Leg.

6. Eyes: Sew on black Eye beads.

7. Tail: Clip a fringe on the Tail, fold, and sew the Tail. Sew Tail on Body.

Giraffe Pattern

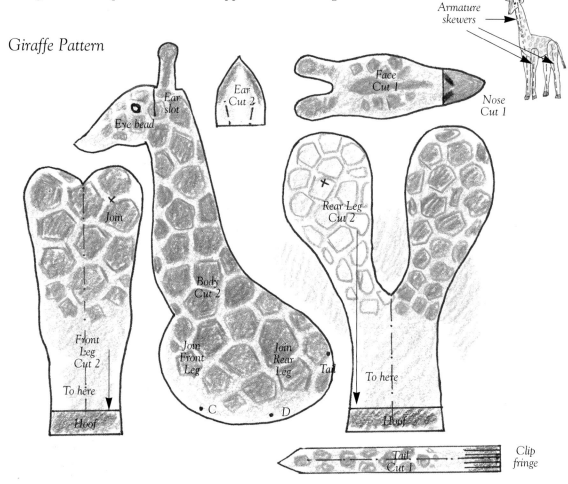

Armature skewers

Ear slot
Eye bead
Ear Cut 2
Face Cut 1
Nose Cut 1

Join
Front Leg Cut 2
To here
Hoof

Body Cut 2
Join Front Leg
Join Rear Leg
Tail
C
D

Rear Leg Cut 2
To here
Hoof

Tail Cut 1
Clip fringe

Mousse, the Moose

This makes a 6" tall moose.

▲ *A moose's horns are called a rack. You'd think the weight would hurt his back!*

Materials

Body: 6" x 9" brown felt
Antlers: 4" x 6" light tan felt
Eyes: Two black beads
Armatures: Bamboo skewers or stove pipe wire, pipe cleaner for antlers
Matching thread, black thread for mouth, strong thread for joints
Polyester stuffing
Buttons for joints: Two 1/2" size and two 7/16" size
Scissors, two needles, stuffing tool

1. Pattern: Trace all pattern pieces on felt. Sew by hand or machine.

2. Make the Moose the same as the Giraffe (page 67) with these exceptions:

A. Antlers: Bend a matching pipe cleaner to fit the antler as marked with a 1/2" loop twisted at the base. Zigzag or whip-stitch over the pipe cleaner into the Antler. Repeat. Sew the Face to the Head, Ear slot to A to Ear slot. Insert the Antler loop ends and pin. Sew Face to Body Ear slot to B to Ear slot.

B. Hoofs: Insert button for joint and sew the Legs 1/4" from the Hoof as marked. Stuff lightly, push in the wrapped armature, and sew on the Hoof. Repeat.

C. No spots.

Moose Pattern

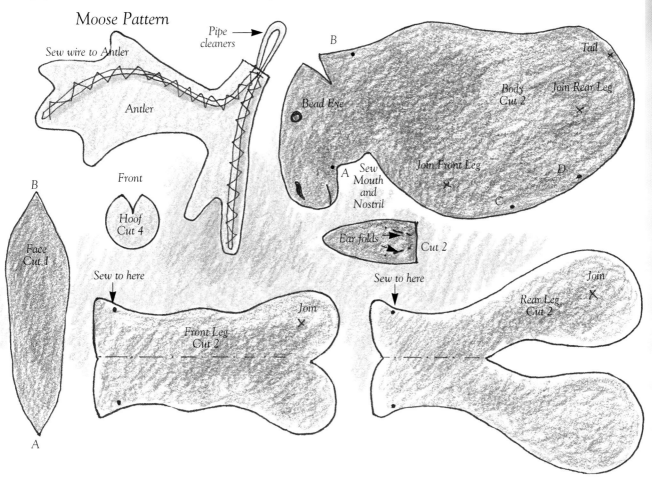

Sew wire to Antler

Pipe cleaners

Antler

Front

Hoof Cut 4

B

Face Cut 1

A

Sew to here

Front Leg Cut 2

Join

B

Bead Eye

A Sew Mouth and Nostril

Tail

Body Cut 2

Join Rear Leg

Join Front Leg

D

C

Ear folds Cut 2

Sew to here

Rear Leg Cut 2

Join

23

Minkey, the Monkey

This pattern makes a 3-1/2" long monkey (plus tail).

▲ *Monkey, monkey in the tree,*
Funny face, you look like me.

Materials

Head, Body, and Legs: 4" x 8" brown felt
Face and Ears: 1-1/2" x 2" tan felt
Hands Feet and Tail: 15" large brown pipe cleaner
   or 3" x 3" tan felt
Eyes: Two 1/8" black beads

Fiberfill stuffing
Matching threads
Black embroidery floss
Vest: 2" x 4" fuchsia felt, 10" gold braid trim
Craft scissors for wires, scissors, needle, stuffing tool

1. Pattern: Cut out all pattern pieces.
2. Body: Align the Body pieces. Whip-stitch from the back Head dart to 1/2" from the Tail joining. Fold back 1/2" of the Tail pipe cleaner, insert it into this seam, and sew firmly. Fold Tail tip back tightly 1/4" to cover wire end. Continue sewing to Head dart. Sew Body front seam.
3. Stuff: Fill the Body very firmly with fiberfill.

2. and 3.

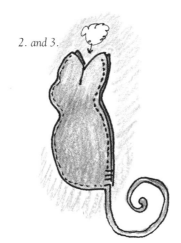

4. Head: Insert Ears, stuff, and sew the Head dart to close.
5. Face: Sew the Chin dart and whip-stitch the Face in place. Use black embroidery floss (two or three strands) to sew on black bead Eyes emerging at the Nose; sew two French knots (see page 12). Sew across the Mouth.

4. and 5.

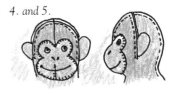

6. Arms, Hands, and Feet:
A. Clip 3" of pipe cleaner. At 1/2" make a 3/4" loop for the Hand or Foot. Fold the other end back 1/4".
B. Fold the Arm over the other end and sew around the 1/2" thumb to hold the Hand (Foot) in place. Sew up the Arm (Leg) to 1/2", stuff firmly, and sew closed. Repeat for all four. Optional: Make felt Hands and Feet.

7. To finish: (See Sewn Joints, page 16 or 27.) Use a strong double thread knotted to join the Arms and Legs.

8. Vest: Use fuchsia felt. Cut out, sew shoulder seams, and top stitch gold braid edging.

8.

7.

6.

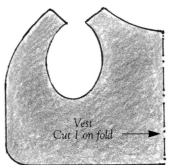

Vest
Cut 1 on fold →

Monkey Pattern

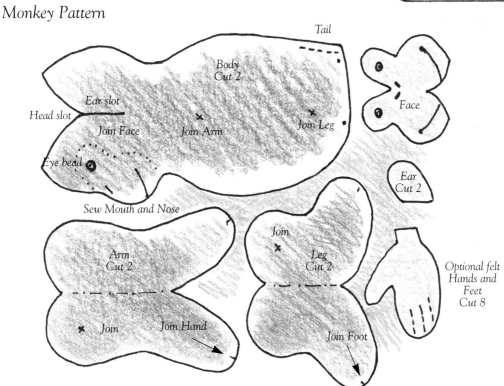

Tail

Body
Cut 2

Ear slot

Head slot

Join Face

Join Arm

Join Leg

Eye bead

Face

Ear
Cut 2

Sew Mouth and Nose

Arm
Cut 2

Join

Join Hand

Leg
Cut 2

Join

Join Foot

Optional felt
Hands and
Feet
Cut 8

24

Honey, the Bee

This pattern makes a 3-3/4" bee.

Have You Thought of This?

For a novel effect, add the bee to a collection of objects for a flower arrangement. Objects include the bee, artificial flowers, the base of a palm branch, and a large sea shell.

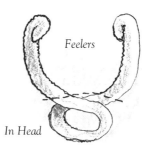

▲ *Find some daisies, buzzy bees
And carry pollen on your knees.*

Materials

Head, Thorax, and Tail: 4" x 6" black felt
Ruff and Body: 5" x 5" yellow fur 1/4" pile
Feet and Feelers: Five 15" black pipe cleaners
Wings: 4" x 10" clear vinyl (cut double or use thick vinyl)

Fiberfill stuffing
Matching threads
Eyes: Two 1/8" sequins
Craft scissors for wires, sharp scissors, needle, sewing machine, stuffing tool

1. Pattern: Cut out all pattern pieces except Wings. For the faux fur, make small snips from the reverse side to avoid cutting the pile.

2. Wings:
A. To hand sew: cut out the Wings (double). Overcast all around each Wing with yellow thread to outline the Wings.
B. To machine sew: Note: Vinyl sticks to the sewing machine. Stack backing paper, clear vinyl (doubled), and the traced pattern. Use yellow thread to straight-stitch around Wings just inside the traced line. Cut out wings outside the traced line. Care-fully tear away papers.

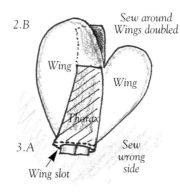

3. Assembling the Bee:(Sew on the reverse side. The Belly seam is left open.)
A. Insert the Wings in the Thorax slots and sew on reverse side.
B. Match the Head pieces and sew the front seam. Turn and

push the seam flat to mold the shape (rounded).
C. Twist the Feelers into shape with a loop on the inside.

D. Align the Ruff with the Head, place the Feelers in the seam, and sew.
E. Match the Thorax to the Ruff and sew.

F. Match the Tail to the Body and sew.

G. Match the Body to the Thorax and sew.

4. Legs: Fold and twist three pipe cleaners together for 1". Clip back Legs at 3-1/2", the other four 2-3/4". Fold 1/2" foot on each.

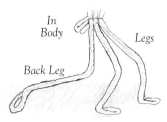

In Body

Legs

Back Leg

5. Turn Bee and sew the Belly seam closed from Tail to Thorax. Insert the Legs and sew the Legs firmly in place. Sew the Thorax and Ruff closed and stuff with fiberfill.

6. To Finish: Sew sequin Eyes on the Head. Bend the Legs to shape.

Bee Pattern

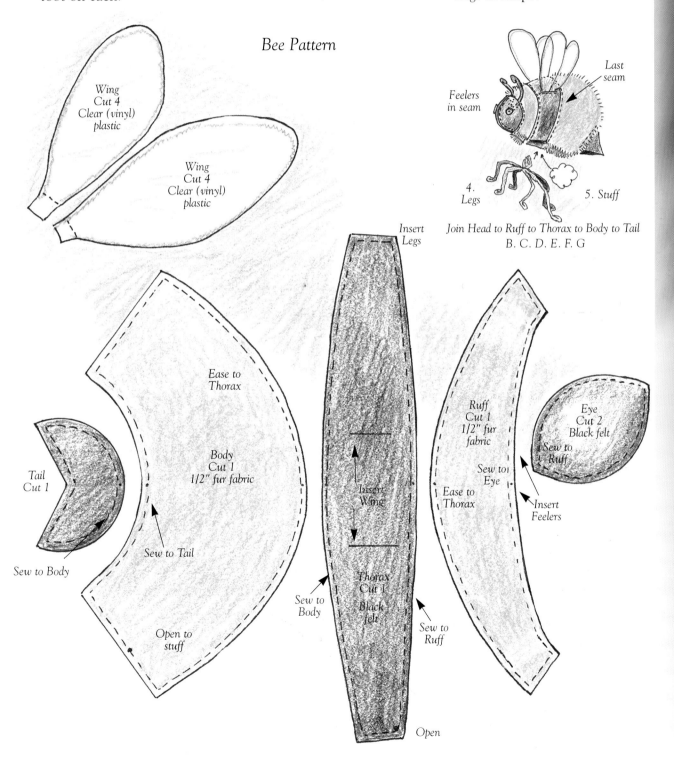

Wing
Cut 4
Clear (vinyl)
plastic

Wing
Cut 4
Clear (vinyl)
plastic

Last seam

Feelers in seam

4.
Legs

5. Stuff

Join Head to Ruff to Thorax to Body to Tail
B. C. D. E. F. G

Ease to Thorax

Body
Cut 1
1/2" fur fabric

Tail
Cut 1

Sew to Tail

Sew to Body

Open to stuff

Insert Legs

Insert Wing

Thorax
Cut 1
Black felt

Sew to Body

Sew to Ruff

Open

Ruff
Cut 1
1/2" fur fabric

Sew to Eye

Ease to Thorax

Insert Feelers

Eye
Cut 2
Black felt

Sew to Ruff

25

Echo, the Bat

This pattern makes a 7" wide bat.
You can add wing hooks if you wish.

▲ *With sonar bats can fly at night.*
We prefer the moon light bright.

Materials

Wings and Ears: 3" x 8" brown felt
Body: 3" x 5" gray/brown berber cloth (a nubby
   fabric)
Feet and Wings: Two brown pipe cleaners
Eyes: Two 1/8" black beads

Fiberfill stuffing
Matching threads
Sewing machine, needle, sharp scissors, craft scis-
   sors, stuffing tool

1. Pattern: Cut out all pattern pieces. For berber cloth, sew from the wrong side.
2. Wings:
A. Mark the pin tucks and the pipe cleaner lines.
B. Fold the Wing back to back at pin tuck lines and top-stitch in 1/8".

2. B

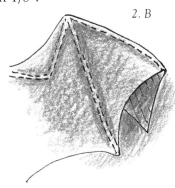

C. Lay the pipe cleaner on the Leg line with 1-1/4" protruding and zigzag over it. Repeat for the Arm if desired.
3. Ears: Tuck the Ear in the Ear slot, align edges face to face, and sew. Repeat.
4. Body: Match Body sides face to face and sew the mid seam. Match the Body to the Back face to face and sew from D around to C. Turn, stuff lightly, and sew closed. Don't clip the thread. Align and sew the Body to the Wing with unclipped matching thread because stitches show on the Wing back.

4.

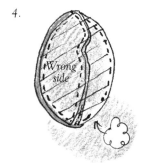

Wrong side

5. To Finish: Sew the black Eye beads on the Head. Double back 1/4" on pipe cleaner ends. Bend hooks to shape.

5.

5.

4.

Bat Pattern

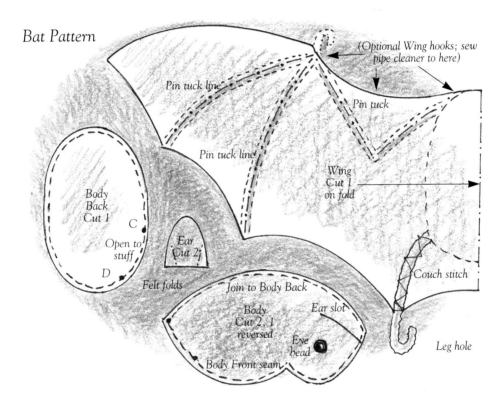

(Optional Wing hooks; sew pipe cleaner to here)

Pin tuck line

Pin tuck

Pin tuck line

Body Back Cut 1

C

Open to stuff

D

Ear Cut 2

Wing Cut 1 on fold

Felt folds

Join to Body Back

Couch stitch

Body Cut 2, 1 reversed

Ear slot

Eye bead

Body Front seam

Leg hole

Have You Thought of This?

An inventive visitor hooked the bat toy's claw into the perforated metal lampshade on my desk. It looked so comfortable that I left it there. Less spooky toys could be arranged to ring the base of a lamp, decorate a cloth lamp shade, or perch on the finial.

26

Barny, the Owl

This pattern makes an owl about 4" tall. With velveteen fabric, sewing by machine makes the sturdiest seams. Baste (if necessary) and finish by hand sewing.

▲ Owls have such nice big eyes. This makes them look so very wise.

Materials

Face and Front: 3-1/2" x 8" white faux fur (1/4" pile)
Body and Wings: 7" x 8" brown velveteen print
Under Wing: 3" x 3-1/2" white satin
Beak: 1" x 2" orange velveteen or suede cloth
Feet: One tan pipe cleaner

Eyes: Two 1/2" brown plastic eyes with post and washer
Fiberfill stuffing and pellets
Matching threads
Sewing machine, sharp scissors, pins, needle, stuffing tool

1. Pattern: Cut out all pattern pieces. Add 1/4" seam allowances for velveteen. On fur, snip carefully from the reverse side. Sew from the reverse side and tuck fur pile out of the seam to sew. Mark Eye placement and cut a slit.

2. Wings:
A. Align Top and Lower Wings face to face and sew the edges with tiny stitches. Turn Wings.
B. Tuck the Wing in the Wing slot, align edges, and sew. Repeat.

3. Beak: Sew the Beak to the Face. It's not easy, so baste first.

4. Face: Fold face to face and sew the Beak and the Neck. Push the Beak with a skewer to turn. Insert the Eye post and push the washer on firmly. Repeat.

5. Join the Face to the Chest.

6. Feet: Twist pipe cleaners into Feet as shown. Tuck the Feet into the Feet slots, feet forward, projection inside, align slot edges, and sew.

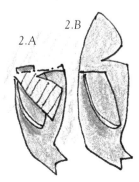

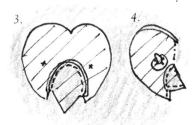

7. Body: Stay-stitch velveteen edges on the C to D opening. Sew Body darts. Align Bodies and sew the back seam to the Tail. Align the Body and Chest matching As. Sew, leaving C to D open on one side. Match the Tail pieces and sew from A to the Tail. Fold the Tail seam to seam and sew across.

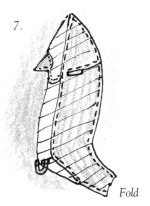

7.

Fold

8. Stuff: Turn the Owl right side out. Fill the Head with fiberfill. Fill the Body with pellets. Sew C to D closed.

7. Tail

8.

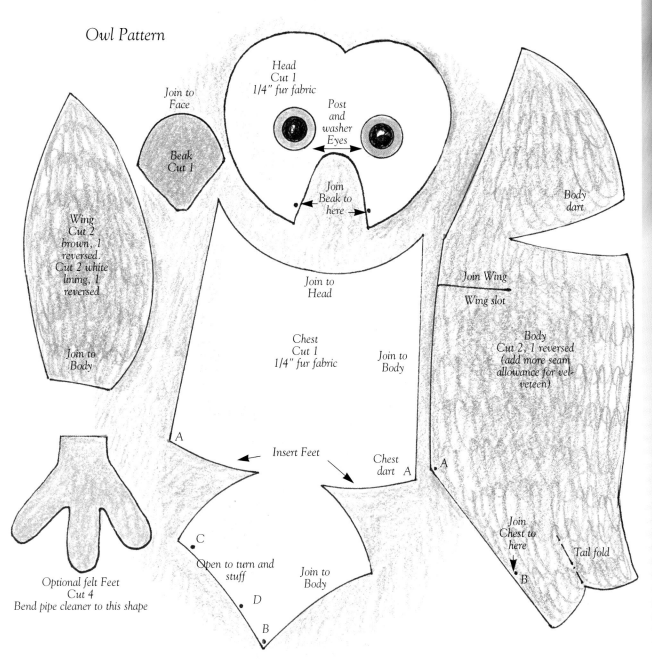

Owl Pattern

Join to Face

Beak Cut 1

Head Cut 1 1/4" fur fabric

Post and washer Eyes

Body dart

Wing Cut 2 brown, 1 reversed. Cut 2 white lining, 1 reversed

Join Beak to here

Join to Body

Join to Head

Join Wing

Wing slot

Body Cut 2, 1 reversed (add more seam allowance for velveteen)

Chest Cut 1 1/4" fur fabric

Join to Body

A

Insert Feet

Chest dart A

A

Optional felt Feet Cut 4 Bend pipe cleaner to this shape

C

Open to turn and stuff

Join to Body

D

B

Join Chest to here

B

Tail fold

27

Polly, the Parrot

*This makes a colorful 6″ tall bird.
For fabric, add seam allowances as
needed. Sew by hand or machine
and finish by hand.*

▲ *Parrots do much more than squawk.
They can even learn to talk.*

Materials

Head: 3″ x 5″ red felt
Body and Under Wing: 5″ x 10″ green felt
Wings: 4″ x 4″ blue felt
Wing color and Under Tail: 4″ x 4″ yellow felt
Beak: 1-1/2″ x 3″ metallic fabric
Feet and Lower Beak: 3″ x 5″ black felt
Eye: 3/4″ x 3/4″ white felt

Eyes: Two 1/2″ green plastic eyes with post and
washer
Fiberfill stuffing
Green (G), black (B), and red (R) thread
Feet armatures: Black pipe cleaners
Needle, craft scissors for pipe cleaners, sharp scis-
sors, stuffing tool

1. Pattern: Cut out all pattern pieces. Mark the Eye
placement and cut a slit. This
is sewn right side out with
felt.
2. Wings: Stack and align
the yellow Wing, blue Top
Wing, and green Lower Wing.
Whip-stitch the edges.
Repeat.
3. Head: Align Head pieces
and sew the Head top. Insert
the Eye post through the
white Eye patch and Head and
push the washer on firmly.
(Insert Eye later for machine-
sewn parrot. The presser foot
will hit the Eye post.)

4. Beak:
A. Lay the metallic Upper
Beak on the Lower Beak.
Satin-stitch across the mouth
to secure (matching thread).
Repeat.
B. Align the Beaks face to
face and sew the upper beak
with firm stitching. Turn.
C. Align the Beak with the
Head opening and sew to join.

3. and 4.

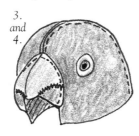

5. Body: Match the Body
pieces and whip-stitch (G)
the back seam from Tail to
Neck. Place the Wings on the
Body as marked and baste.
6. Assemble the bird:
A. Align the Head with the
Body and sew, including
Wings.
B. Fold the Head to align the
Beak and Neck seam and sew
(B) from the tip of the Beak
to the Neck. Sew (R) the
Neck. Sew (G) down the front
of the Body.

C. Align the Under Tail with the Body and sew (G) from D around to the Leg. Sew between the Legs. Sew the other Leg to C and leave open.

5. and 6.

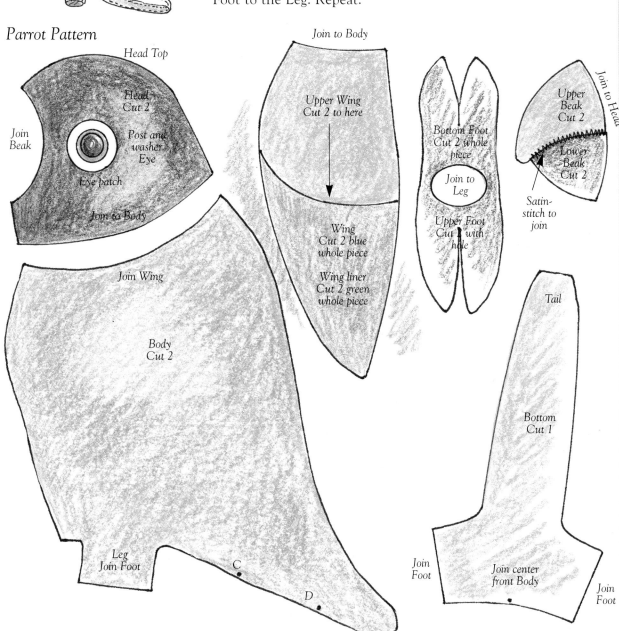

6.C

7. Feet:
A. Twist the pipe cleaners into Feet smaller than the felt Feet with 2" Leg wire left over. Align upper and lower felt Feet and sew (B) the edges around the pipe cleaner armature. Repeat.
B. Insert the Leg pipe cleaner into the Body. Repeat.

8. Stuff: Fill the bird with fiberfill, Beak first. Sew C to D closed.

9. Finish: Whip-stitch the Foot to the Leg. Repeat.

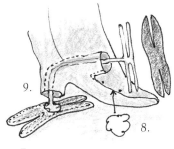

9.

7.

8.

Parrot Pattern

Head Top

Head Cut 2

Join Beak

Post and washer Eye

Eye patch

Join to Body

Join Wing

Body Cut 2

Leg Join Foot

C

D

Join to Body

Upper Wing Cut 2 to here

Wing Cut 2 blue whole piece

Wing liner Cut 2 green whole piece

Bottom Foot Cut 2 whole piece

Join to Leg

Upper Foot Cut 2 with hole

Upper Beak Cut 2

Lower Beak Cut 2

Satin-stitch to join

Join to Head

Tail

Bottom Cut 1

Join Foot

Join center front Body

Join Foot

28

Benjie, the Penguin

This makes a 6" tall penguin, sewn here by machine from the reverse side with very narrow seam allowances.

▲ *Penguins waddle in the breeze*
But swim like fish when under seas.

Materials

Body: 6" x 10" black felt, shiny fabric, or short fur
Muzzle: 6" x 9" white felt, shiny fabric, or fur
Color: 1" x 3" yellow felt
Eyes: Two post and washer 7mm plastic eyes, yellow and black

Matching thread
Polyester stuffing, pellet stuffing
Sewing machine or hand sewing needle, stuffing tool, sharp scissors, funnel

1. Pattern: Cut out each piece singly. Mark the Eye slit.
2. Head: Match the Color to the Head and seam. Repeat. Insert the Eye post and push the washer firmly in place. Match the Head pieces and sew from the Beak tip to Neck back on the reverse side.
3. Added pieces: Match black and white Flipper, sew, and turn. Repeat. Match two Feet pieces and seam the edges. Repeat.
4. Body: Match Body pieces and sew the back seam from the Neck to the Tail. Place Wings on the Body as marked and baste.
5. Belly: Align the Belly to the Body and sew the edges together, including the Flipper. Repeat.
6. Match Belly pieces. Sew from the Beak tip to the Belly bottom.
7. Place the Feet on the bottom, ease to fit 3/4" for each foot, and baste. Match the bottom to the Body and sew, including the Feet in this seam. Leave C to D open to turn and stuff.
8. Turn and stuff the Beak, Head, and Neck with fiberfill. Fill the Body with pellets. Sew the opening closed.

7.

Penguin Pattern

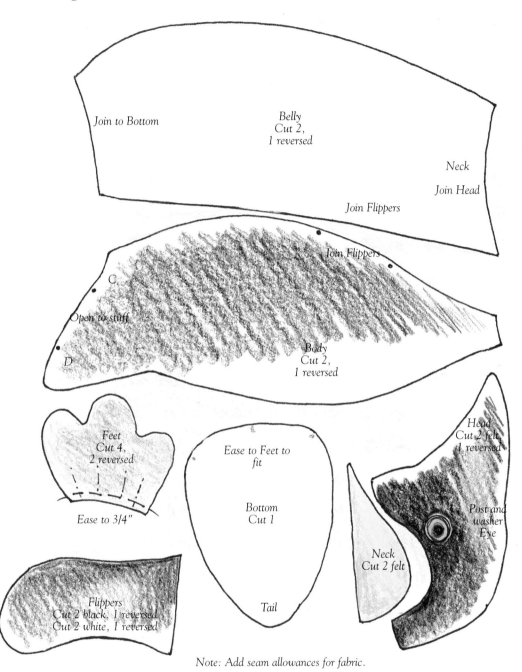

Join to Bottom

Belly
Cut 2,
1 reversed

Neck
Join Head

Join Flippers

Join Flippers

C

Open to stuff

D

Body
Cut 2,
1 reversed

Feet
Cut 4,
2 reversed

Ease to 3/4"

Ease to Feet to
fit

Bottom
Cut 1

Tail

Head
Cut 2 felt,
1 reversed

Post and
washer
Eye

Neck
Cut 2 felt

Flippers
Cut 2 black, 1 reversed
Cut 2 white, 1 reversed

Note: Add seam allowances for fabric.

Ian Goodrich holds two fish.
He enjoys the weight of
their pellet stuffing.

What's Inside

Chapter 6

◄ Emily Goodrich and
Charming, the Frog.

Stuffing

Most of the toys in Chapters 1 to 5 are firmly stuffed and have rotating joints. This mechanism comes from porcelain dolls with jointed arms and legs. Early Raggedy Ann dolls and teddy bears were packed to stiffness with wood shavings called excelsior. This stuffing made use of waste wood products and toys lasted well—until moths ate the wood into sawdust and the dolly or teddy flattened.

Nowadays, many toys are designed to be floppy. The shape is built into the pattern and the toys flop naturally—well, not too naturally. The pellets all flow to the bottom and the head remains empty. So the best stuffing for these toys is a combination of fiberfill for heads, hands, horns (parts that would look odd flat) and shifting pellets for the rest. Throughout this book, toy patterns all tell how to stuff them, what kind of stuffing to use, and where to stuff them. All are marked with a C to D opening to stuff (and turn) which fits a funnel tip.

Fiberfill

This commonly available synthetic stuffing is washable, non-allergenic, fairly inexpensive, and easy to use. Fiberfill toys can be packed firmly or loosely; however, rotating joints do not work well with soft stuffing. To stuff with fiberfill, sculpture the toy bit by bit using small wads poked into the toy by hand or with a tool. Good stuffing tools include wooden rods, bamboo skewers, or your sewing machine screw driver.

Pellets

Materials on-hand, like beans, lentils, macaroni, sand, and potpourri, filled many early floppy toys. The newer polypropylene pellets, found in crafts and fabric stores, are small enough to shift like a bean bag yet are big enough to find when they spill. These pellets are washable, non-toxic, weighted, and easy to use. To stuff with pellets:

1. Sew the toy and stuff the head, feet, tail, etc. as needed with fiberfill.

2. Put the toy in a baking pan or box to catch spills with the C to D slot open.

3. Insert a funnel tip in the slot. Shake the toy and redirect the funnel until the toy is nearly full of pellets. Poke with the skewer to make pellets flow into the toy.

4. Pin the toy opening closed to judge the right amount of stuffing, then add more or shake some out.

5. Sew the opening closed with a hidden whip-stitch over edges folded inward.

6. Use the funnel to pour the rest of the pellets back in the bag.

Assembling Toys

Joining a small leg to a toy is difficult because the small round opening just won't fit in the sewing machine (which does straight seams best). As a rule, toy patterns in this book are designed for the easiest seams to avoid these difficult joinings. Construction of the Lamb, following, shows how to make straight seam joinings on narrow parts such as legs. The idea is to join the narrow sections first, then sew the side seams. However, the toy must be assembled in the order shown for this to work. The following photos show how this works.

Wooly, the Lamb

This pattern makes a 5-1/2" lamb. Because seams are so small, construction is unusual. The legs are joined during the stitching of the body seams. It is important to follow these directions.

▲ *Mary had a little lamb. It grew up to be a ram.*

Materials

Body: 8" x 16" nubby short pile polyester fur fabric
Legs, Ears, and Muzzle: 4" x 8" black suede cloth or velvet
Eyes: Two small black beads

Matching thread
Polyester stuffing, pellet stuffing
Sewing machine or hand sewing needle, stuffing tool, sharp scissors

1. Pattern: Copy the pattern on paper, pin it on fabric, and cut out each piece singly. For fur fabric, make small snips to avoid clipping off the fur. Follow the unusual assembly instructions carefully.

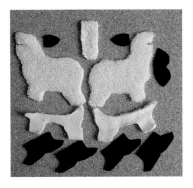

2. Ears: Fold the felt Ear in half and put the Ear in the Ear slot, fold forward. Fold the slot over the Ear and sew from the reverse side.

3. Body: Align the Body pieces and sew from the Nose to the Tail using white or clear monofilament thread. Tuck fur out of the seam.

4. Muzzle: Align the Muzzle to the Head and sew.

5. Tail: Sew the Tail and turn using a tool such as your sewing machine screw driver or a bamboo skewer. Knitting needles or scissor tips are too sharp for turning tools.

6. Under Body: Baste the turned Tail to the rear Under Body edge. Join Under Body pieces and sew, leaving C to D open to turn and stuff.

7. Join the Under Body to the Body at the rear only from Leg to Leg. Stop! (Don't rush ahead and sew the whole Body at this point.)

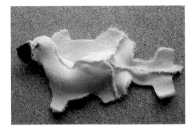

8. Sew the rear Feet to the Body. Stop!

9. Fold the Legs and Feet to align the Hooves. Align the Under Body to the Body and sew to the front Leg ends. You need to switch to black thread for the Feet.

10. Join the front Feet to the Body front Legs as in Step 8.

11. Match the Body and Feet seams and sew to the Muzzle. Switch to black or clear thread. Match the Muzzle edges and sew.

12. To make the divided Hoof, lay the Foot flat.

(Over)

13. Sew (B) the Leg front seam in black or clear thread. To align the Hoof bottom edges, push the Foot tip to the Leg fold. Sew across the Hoof bottom. Repeat for each Leg and Hoof. Turn the Lamb right side out using a blunt turning tool.

14. To stuff the Lamb, firmly pack fiberfill in the Legs until they are stiff enough to stand.

15. To finish, whip-stitch the opening closed. If the Hoof spreads too much, sew a few stitches at the top of the split.

16. Use embroidery floss to sew the Lamb's Nose and Mouth. Sew on two black beads for Eyes.

▼ *Emily Goodrich encourages her favorite Tiny Lamb to try a mouth full of white sand.*

17. If you skipped sewing the Leg darts (because they are difficult) and the Legs splay out, as with the Polar Bear (page 135), sew the Leg darts when the toy is stuffed, pulling the thread tightly to draw the legs to the body.

Lamb Pattern

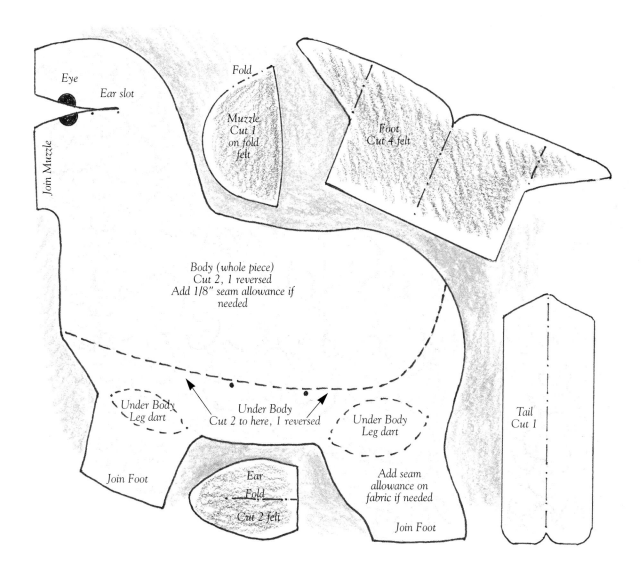

Eye

Ear slot

Join Muzzle

Fold

Muzzle
Cut 1
on fold
felt

Foot
Cut 4 felt

Body (whole piece)
Cut 2, 1 reversed
Add 1/8" seam allowance if
needed

Tail
Cut 1

Under Body
Leg dart

Under Body
Cut 2 to here, 1 reversed

Under Body
Leg dart

Join Foot

Ear
Fold
Cut 2 felt

Add seam
allowance on
fabric if needed

Join Foot

30

Flump, the Walrus

This makes a 6" long walrus. The darker gray walrus on the left is felt. The same pattern was used for the larger walrus, but it was made with a stretchy fabric which fills up fatter.

▲ *The walrus lazes on the shore,*
Flaps a flipper, snorts a snore.

Materials

Body: 8" x 15" gray suede cloth or felt
Muzzle: 1" x 2" gray fur
Tusks: 2" x 4" white felt
Eyes: Two small black beads

Matching thread
Polyester stuffing, pellet stuffing
Sewing machine or hand sewing needle, stuffing
   tool, sharp scissors, funnel

Fabrics: Use flat fabric or felt sewn by hand or machine. Sew on the reverse side. Stuff with a combination of fiberfill and pellets.

1. Pattern: Cut out each pattern piece singly.

2. Tusks: Fold the Tusk, sew, and turn. Repeat. Stuff and join the Tusks to the Muzzle and sew.

3. Flippers: Fold the Front Flipper, sew, and turn. Top-stitch the Flipper Toes. Rear Flipper: Fold the Rear Body Flipper and sew to A. Turn and top-stitch. Repeat.

4. Body: Baste the Front Flippers on the Body. Align Body pieces and sew from the Back Flippers to the Muzzle.

5. Belly: Align the Belly to the Body and sew including the Front Flippers in this seam. Leave C to D open to turn. Sew gathering stitches

on the Neck and pull to wrinkle the Neck.

6. Turn and stuff the Head with fiberfill. Insert the funnel in the C to D slot and fill with pellets. Work over a box to catch errant pellets.

7. Finish: Sew closed. Sew on a black Eye bead. Sew through the Head to the second Eye bead. Sew back to the first Eye. Pull the thread to seat the Eyes and sew a knot. This stitching helps anchor the Head stuffing in place. Sew a black thread across the Muzzle vertically.

Black thread

Top stitch Flippers

Walrus Pattern

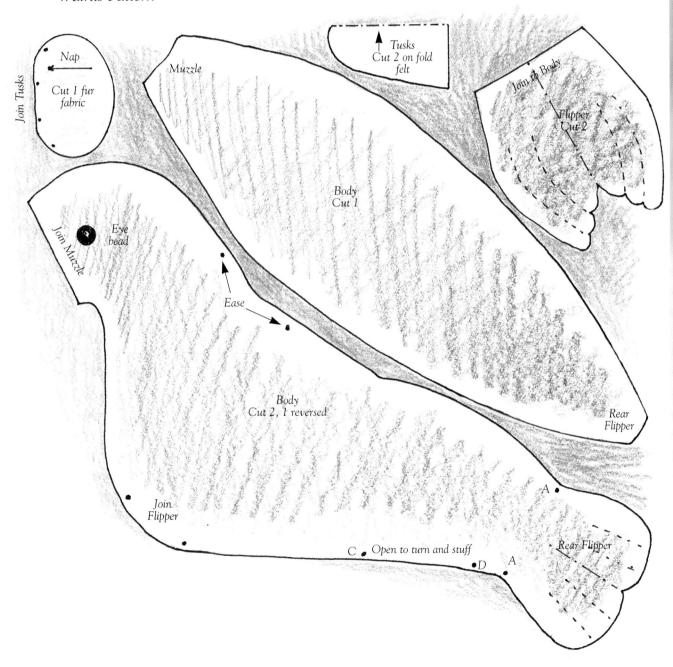

Join Tusks

Nap

Cut 1 fur fabric

Muzzle

Tusks Cut 2 on fold felt

Join to Body

Flipper Cut 2

Join Muzzle

Eye bead

Body Cut 1

Ease

Rear Flipper

Body Cut 2, 1 reversed

Join Flipper

C *Open to turn and stuff*

A

D *A*

Rear Flipper

31

Charming, the Frog

This pattern, sewn from fabric and turned, makes a 5" frog. The challenge here is turning the frog.

▲ *Froggie would a'courting go.*
He may become a prince, you know.

Materials

Body: 4" x 10" lightweight polyester knit with printed metallic design overlaid or two 4-1/2" x 7" pieces
Eyes: Four beads, two large white 1/4" and two green

Matching thread
Stuffing pellets
Sewing machine or hand sewing needle, sharp scissors, funnel, small screw driver or bamboo skewer

The following directions are for non-fray lightweight fabric sewn by machine and filled with shifting pellets. For felt, sew right side out.

1. Pattern: Do not cut out the pattern. Copy the pattern on paper.
2. Sewing: Using a short stitch (1mm), sew the Head darts. Align the frog Top with the Belly.
3. Lay sew top face to face on Belly fabric. Position the paper pattern and pin outside the stitch line or across it. The paper acts as both a sewing guide and fabric stabilizer. Begin at C and sew around to D, leaving an opening to stuff

and turn. Remove the pins and carefully tear off the needle perforated paper. Be careful not to pull stitches out.

Sew through the pattern paper and two layers of face-to-face fabric. Trim after sewing.

4. Trim: Cut out 1/8" outside the stitch line. Use sharp scissors to clip the seam allowances at inside corners.
5. Turn: Pull fabrics apart

and push the Nose seam into the Head. Use the skewer to gently push the Head through the opening and carefully push the Legs right side out. It's not easy, so keep trying. Note: Felt does not need turning.
6. Stuff: Insert the funnel and pour pellets into the frog. Poke pellets with the skewer and shake the toy to work pellets into legs. Stuff until full but not bulging.
7. Finish: Sew the opening closed. Sew a knot. Sew a white Eye bead through the green Eye bead and back though the white bead. Emerge at the other eye. Repeat.

Have You Thought of This?

Letter your own greeting card and tie a small animal onto it with a narrow ribbon: "Hoppy Birthday!" with the Frog, "Halo, Friend!" with the Angel, or whatever pun suits your occasion.

3.

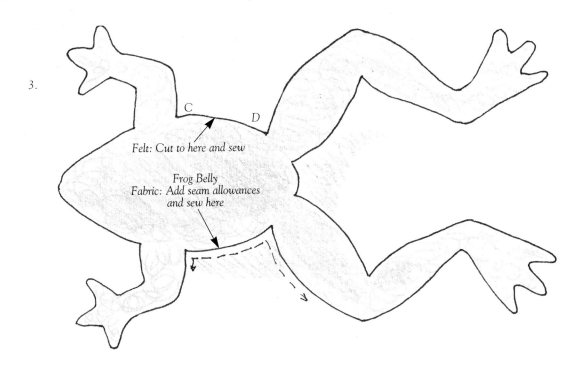

C   D

Felt: Cut to here and sew

Frog Belly
Fabric: Add seam allowances
and sew here

Frog Pattern

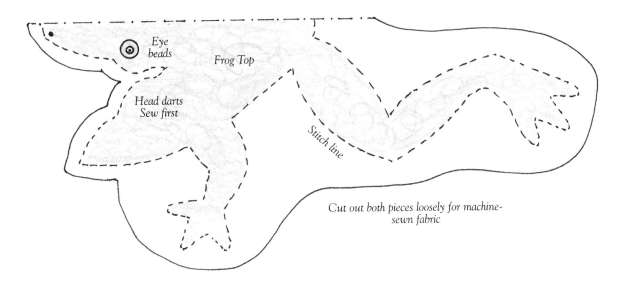

Eye
beads

Frog Top

Head darts
Sew first

Stitch line

Cut out both pieces loosely for machine-
sewn fabric

32

Sarah Sota, the Red Snapper

▲ *Sequined scales that look most arty*
Dress this fishy for a party.

This pattern makes a 5-1/2" long fish. (Better throw him back—it's too small to keep!) The pattern is designed for non-fray lightweight decorative fabric to be sewn wrong side out by machine and stuffed with shifting pellets. Use paper or stabilizer under the fabric in the sewing machine if needed. The pattern can also be made of felt, sewn right side out, and stuffed with fiberfill. (See Frog pattern, page 90, for details.)

Materials

Body: 7" x 8" polyester knit with printed metallic design overlaid
Fins: 3" x 4" gold metallic
Eyes: Two beads or 6mm plastic toy Eyes with post and washer

Matching thread, gold metallic thread
Fiberfill stuffing and pellets
Paper or stabilizer
Sewing machine or hand sewing needle, sharp scissors, funnel, stuffing tool

1. Pattern: Cut out the pattern pieces with 1/8" or more seam allowances. Mark the Eye hole.

2. Fold four Fins face to face, sew, and turn.

3. Fold the Body dart over the side Fins and sew.

4. Pair the ventral Fins and pin them on the Body, ends outward. Align the Bodies face to face, begin at C, and sew around fish to D, leaving an opening to stuff and turn. Remove the pins and tear off any paper used. Clip the inside corners on the Fins and Tail.

5. Eye: Clip a tiny hole and push the Eye post out the hole. Push the locking washer in place. Repeat.

6. Turn the Fish. Top-stitch across the Dorsal and Ventral Fins. Zigzag across the Tail Fin. Sew a Fin pattern as indicated on the pattern with metallic thread.

7. Put fiberfill into the Mouth area. Top-stitch the Mouth. Fill the Fish with pellets.

8. Finish: Use a blind-stitch or whip-stitch to sew the opening closed, edges tucked inward.

Red Snapper Pattern

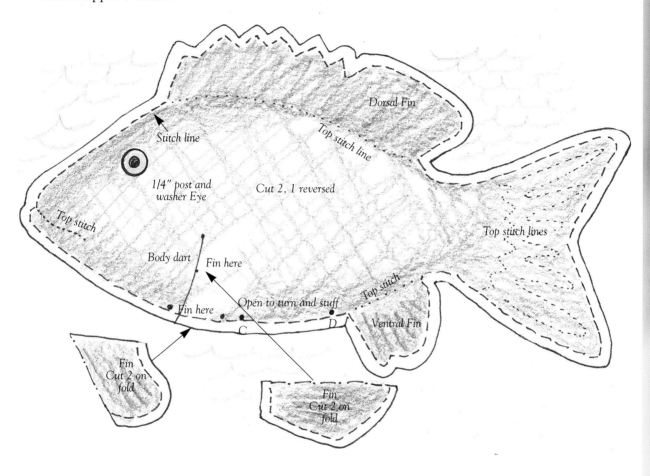

Stitch line

Dorsal Fin

Top stitch line

1/4" post and
washer Eye

Cut 2, 1 reversed

Top stitch

Top stitch lines

Body dart

Fin here

Open to turn and stuff

Top stitch

Fin here

C

D

Ventral Fin

Fin
Cut 2 on
fold

Fin
Cut 2 on
fold

33

Sally, the Salamander

This makes a 7" long skinny salamander. This pattern is designed for non-fray light- weight decorative fabric to be sewn by machine and stuffed with a combination of fiberfill and pellets. The pattern can also be made of felt and stuffed with fiberfill.

▲ *The salamander's called a newt. Its wiggly walk is very cute.*

Materials

Body: 9" x 9" lightweight polyester knit with printed metallic design
Eyes: Four large beads, two orange and two black
Matching thread
Fiberfill stuffing, pellets
Sewing machine or hand sewing needle, small screw driver or bamboo skewer, sharp scissors, funnel

Sew, trim, turn, and stuff the same as for the Frog (page 90) except for these changes:
The Newt has no Body darts. Clip seam allowances at inside corners as shown. Turn. Stuff Head with fiberfill. Sew on orange and black Eye beads.

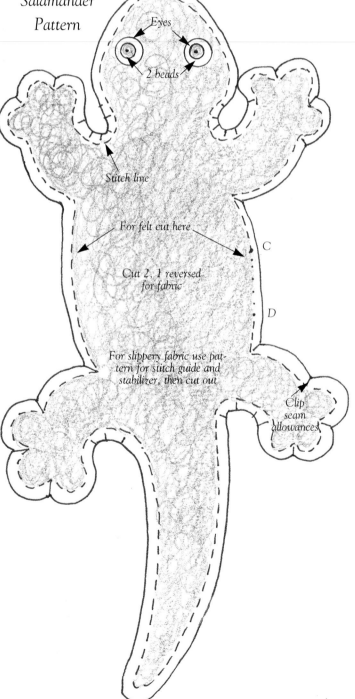

Salamander Pattern

Eyes

2 beads

Stitch line

For felt cut here

C

Cut 2, 1 reversed for fabric

D

For slippery fabric use pat- tern for stitch guide and stabilizer, then cut out

Clip seam allowances

Celeste, the Angel Fish

Makes a 5" long fish. This pattern is designed for non-fray lightweight decorative fabric to be sewn by machine and stuffed with shifting pellets. The pattern can also be made of felt, sewn right side out, and stuffed with fiberfill.

Materials

Body: 7" x 9" polyester knit with printed metallic design overlaid
Fins: 3" x 4" metallic
Eyes: Two beads or 6mm plastic toy Eyes with post and washer
Matching thread, gold metallic thread
Fiberfill stuffing and pellets
Paper or stabilizer
Sewing machine or hand sewing needle, sharp scissors, funnel, stuffing tool

▲ "I am a jewel of the sea.
Don't you wish you looked like me?"

Make the Angel Fish the same way as the Red Snapper (page 92) except for the Tail.
Tail: Sew the Tail, turn and topstitch the lines. Insert the Tail between the Body pieces, sew the Body, and turn.

Angel Fish Pattern

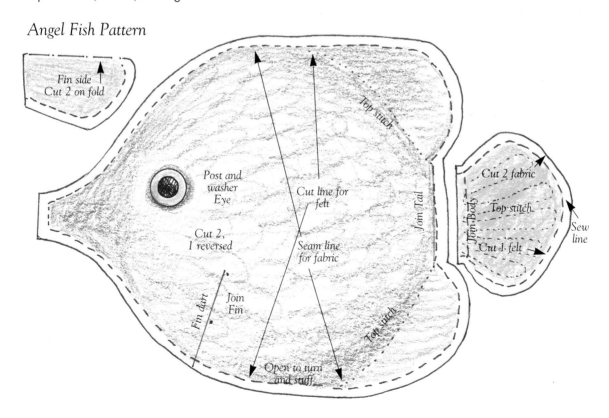

Fin side ↑
Cut 2 on fold

Post and washer Eye

Cut 2,
1 reversed

Cut line for felt

Seam line for fabric

Top stitch

Join Tail

Fin dart

Join Fin

Open to turn and stuff

Top stitch

Cut 2 fabric

Top stitch

Join Body

Cut 1 felt

Sew line

Beau, the Boa Constrictor

Uncoiled, this snake measures 30" long; however, it will always coil when dropped due to the design of the spiral-cut pattern. This pattern is designed for non-fray lightweight decorative fabric to be sewn by machine and stuffed with a combination of fiberfill and pellets.

▲ *This snake can loop into a ring, Then he can hug like anything!*

Materials

Body: 8-1/2" x 17" lightweight polyester knit velour with printed design or two 8-1/2" x 8-1/2" pieces
Eyes: Two large black beads
Matching thread

Polyester stuffing, pellet stuffing
Sewing machine or hand sewing needle, stuffing tool, sharp scissors, funnel

Make the snake the same as the Frog (page 90) with attention to these details:

1. Lay the copied paper pattern on the double fabric and pin outside or across the stitch line. Cut out the tongue and position it inside the Head across the seam line.

2. Sewing: Set the machine to a very short stitch and begin at C near the Head to sew all around to D, the opening, to stuff and turn. Remove the pins and tear off the paper.

3. Trimming: Cut out the Boa, trimming carefully between the stitch lines. Reinforce any stitching if the seam allowance is too narrow.

4. Turning the boa: Pull the fabric apart at the Tail. Use a long rod to push the Tail through the Body. Avoid piling up fabric. Keep on pushing the Tail in and pulling the fabric over the turned fabric on the skewer. When the tip emerges pull to turn. Turn the head.

5. Stuff: Use the skewer to poke fiberfill into the head. Pour pellets into the Boa and sew closed.

6. Eyes: Sew on black Eye beads, sewing through the Head stuffing to anchor.

Boa Pattern

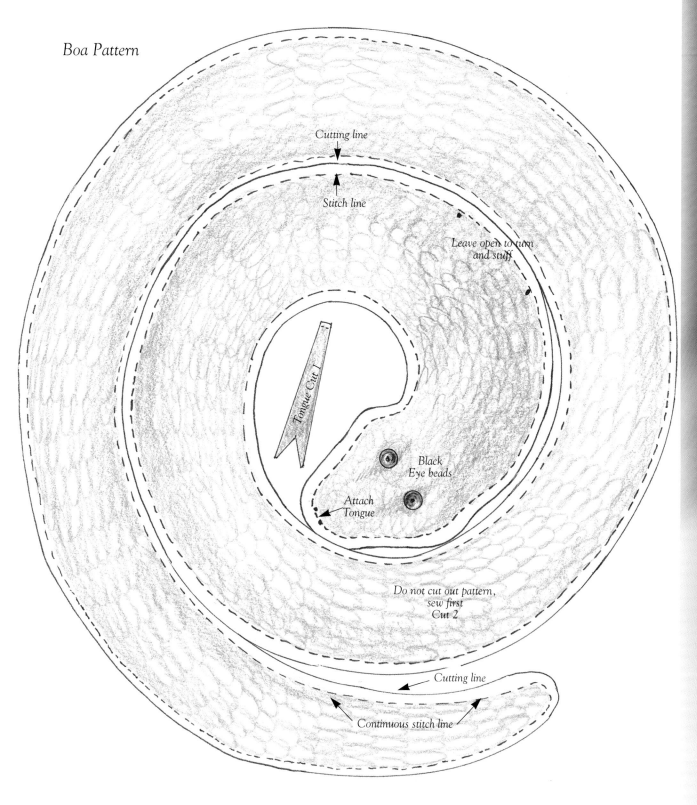

Cutting line

Stitch line

Leave open to turn
and stuff

Tongue Cut 1

Black
Eye beads

Attach
Tongue

Do not cut out pattern,
sew first
Cut 2

Cutting line

Continuous stitch line

Have You Thought of This?

A boa is meant to be worn, isn't it? Etsuko Sato Vosburg wears a velvety toy boa constrictor as jewelry on a simple woven dress.

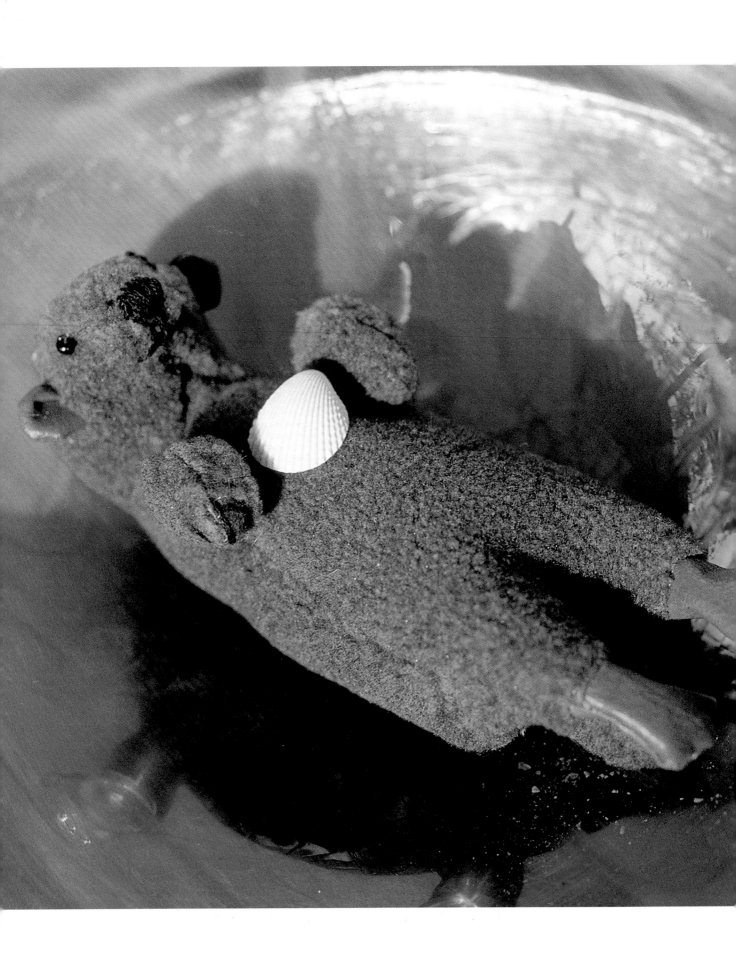

Bean Bag Toys

Chapter 7

Size and Scale

Every toy designer has a concept in mind when creating patterns. Mine is to honor the characteristics of real animals or people. Beanie Baby toys are based on these characteristics, too, emphasizing animal babies which are more round and cute than adults. For success, shapes and materials of toys need to be in proper proportion. Brown Bear (page 100) is made from a bulky knitted fleece and the pattern has some tight corners so he is larger than Tiny Teddy (page 14). You will be grateful for the increased size when sewing furry fabrics.

Scale is important on small toys. The 1/8" fur on a 5" bear would be about 7-1/2" long on a 5' bear because he's twelve times bigger. A 1/2" pile fabric would equal half of a foot times 5, making 30" fur—a very fat bear, indeed. Volume and weight increase, too. A 5" toy full of pellets is light enough for a baby to play with, but would be a hulking giant at five feet tall. This one-ounce toy would weigh 12 x 12 x 12 or over 100 pounds!

This background is handy if you plan to make changes, use unusual fabrics, or scale up the pattern to a larger size. For more on this, the next chapter takes you through steps to help design your own toys.

Sewing Fur Fabrics

1. Fur fabric, napped fabrics, and velveteen, like real fur, have a nap or direction in which the fur lies. Think of petting a dog or cat—you naturally stroke with the fur direction. An arrow on the pattern indicates nap direction to lay out pattern pieces. This makes a difference.

2. To cut pile fabric, trace the pattern on the reverse side and make tiny snips to avoid clipping off the fur pile.

3. To sew fur, brush or tuck the pile out of the seam. Use a long pin, the point of closed embroidery scissors, or a new metal finger-tip tool to keep tucking the fur out of the seam as you sew.

4. Flick closed scissors back and forth across pile stuck in seams to dislodge and pry fibers out with the pin.

5. Not all fur on an animal is the same length. Give the toy a trim to look right. Clip as the barbers do across the upright fur to get an even length (see the Polar Bear, page 135). Muzzles, faces, and feet are most apt to be in need of a shaping trim. Patterns specify trimming.

36

Barry, the Brown Bear

This somewhat complicated pattern makes a 5" tall bear. Use a short pile fabric and sew by machine with hand sewn details and stuff with a combination of fiberfill and pellets. Sew on the reverse side.

▲ *Bears have flat feet as people do*
So they can run as fast as you!

Materials

Body: 8" x 16" berber cloth, a dense short pile polyester fur fabric
Ears and Tail: 1" x 2" brown felt
Eyes: Two small black beads
Matching thread

Polyester stuffing, pellet stuffing
Sewing machine or hand sewing needle, stuffing tool;, sharp scissors, funnel

1. Pattern: Cut out the pattern pieces.

2. Added pieces: Sew Ears and Tail with a tiny seam allowance and turn. Sew the Ears in the Ear slot. Sew the Head darts. Baste the Tail to E on the lower Chest. Don't sew the Chest slit on the Chest.

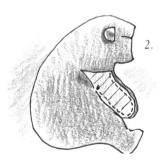

3. Arm: Match the inner Arm with the Body Arm and

sew from the neck around the Paw to the Arm Pit A. Fold the Arm Flap down and sew it to the Body toward the Leg. Repeat for the other side.

4. Body: Align the Chest with the Body, matching all of the Legs. Sew from the Foot Toe to the Muzzle and repeat for the other side. Sew the Feet on the Legs. Sew from the Heel, including the Tail, to the opposite Heel, leaving C to D open.

5. Muzzle: Sew the Muzzle to the Head. Fold the Muzzle and sew from the Nose to the end of the Chest slit.

6. Sew the Inner Leg darts.

7. Stuff: Turn and stuff the Muzzle and Head with fiberfill. Funnel in the pellets. Sew C to D closed.

8. Finish: For the Eyes, sew on small black beads, sewing through the Head stuffing. Use black embroidery floss or two beads to sew a Nose. Sew a Mouth and Claws.

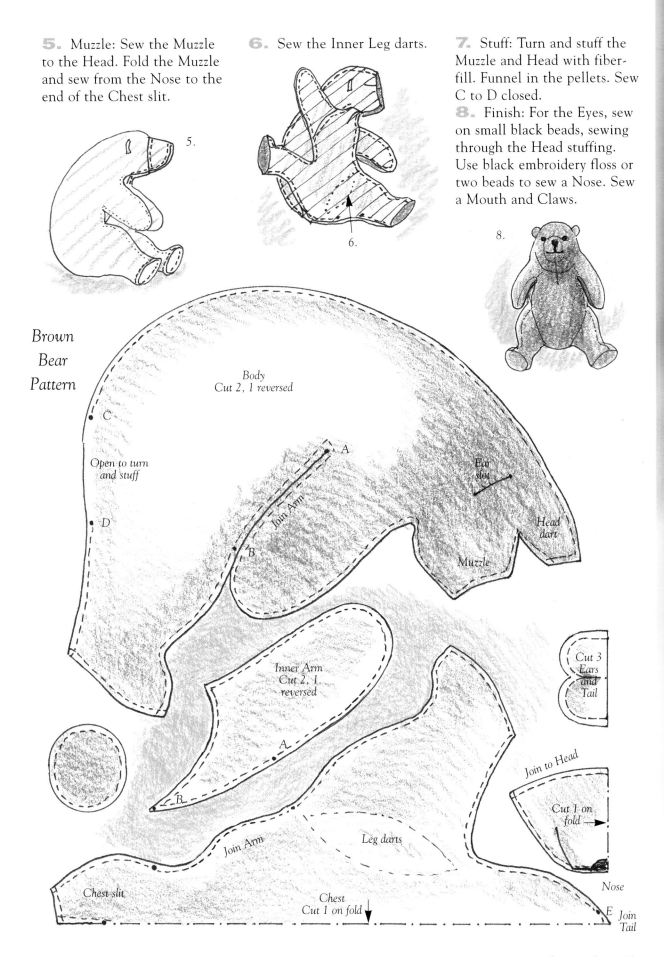

5.

6.

8.

Brown
Bear
Pattern

Body
Cut 2, 1 reversed

• C

Open to turn
and stuff

• D

A

Join Arm

• B

Ear
slot

Head
dart

Muzzle

Inner Arm
Cut 2, 1
reversed

A

B

Join Arm

Leg darts

Cut 3
Ears
and
Tail

Join to Head

Cut 1 on
fold

Chest slit

Chest
Cut 1 on fold

Nose

E Join
Tail

37

Frankenfurter, the Dachshund

Makes a 5-1/2" long dog.

▲ *Longs legs, short back, and turned out toes,*
The dachshund looks down his long nose.

Materials

Body: 8" x 16" felt or short pile polyester fur fabric
Eyes: Two small black beads
Matching thread

Polyester stuffing, pellet stuffing
Sewing machine or hand sewing needle, stuffing
tool, sharp scissors, funnel

1. Pattern: Cut out pattern pieces.
2. Added pieces: For fabric, sew Ears double and turn. Sew the Tail, turn, and stuff lightly with pellets.
3. Body: Align the Body pieces and sew from the Chest A to the Nose B. Sew from the Ear slot to Tail E.
4. Head: Match the Face to the Head and sew from B to the Ear slot. Repeat.
5. Ears: Fold the Ear, tuck it fold forward in the Ear slot and sew. Repeat.

6. Under Body:
A. Sew the Leg darts.
B. Baste the Tail on the Under Body end. Match the Under Body pieces and sew the center seam, leaving open from C to D to turn and stuff.
7. Legs: Align the Under Body to Body and sew.
8. Turn. Stuff the Head and Feet with fiberfill. Fill the Body with pellets and sew the opening closed.

9. Finish: Sew on bead Eyes, sewing through the Head stuffing. Use black embroidery floss to sew the mouth and sew on the felt Nose. Use brown thread to sew Claws. Pull thread tightly to shape the paws.

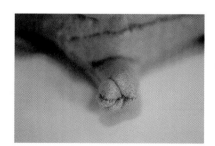

Dachshund Pattern

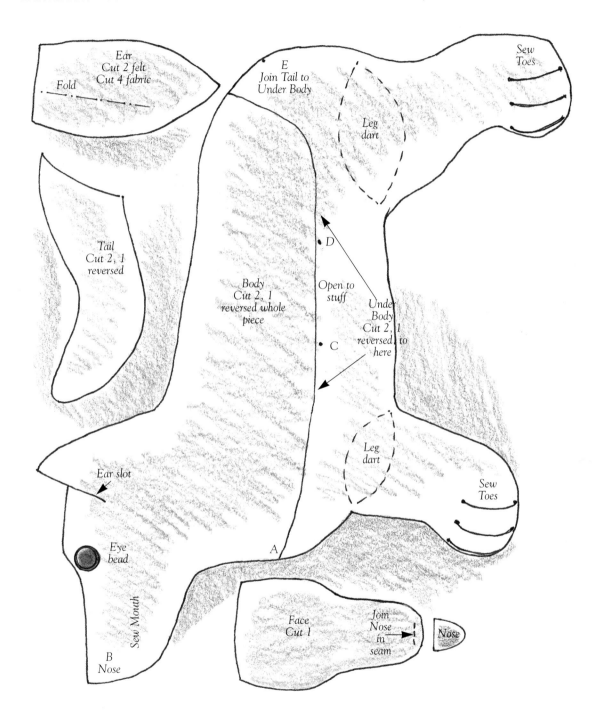

Ear
Cut 2 felt
Cut 4 fabric

Fold

E
Join Tail to
Under Body

Leg
dart

Sew
Toes

Tail
Cut 2, 1
reversed

D

Open to
stuff

Under
Body
Cut 2, 1
reversed, to
here

Body
Cut 2, 1
reversed whole
piece

C

Leg
dart

Sew
Toes

Ear slot

Eye
bead

A

Sew Mouth

Face
Cut 1

Join
Nose
in
seam

Nose

B
Nose

38

Aromaly, the Skunk

Makes a 5" long skunk, plus a 4" tail. Be sure to brush fur out of the seams when sewing and sew wrong side out.

▲ *When skunks get in an angry spell
They lift their tails and shoot off smell.*

Materials

Body: 7" x 12" black fur fabric (1/4")
Under Body: 4" x 5" black suede cloth
Stripe: 3" x 6" white faux fur fabric
Ears: 1" x 2" black or brown felt
Eyes: Two small black beads

Matching thread
Polyester stuffing, pellet stuffing
Sewing machine or hand sewing needle, stuffing
    tool, sharp scissors, funnel

1. Pattern: Cut out pattern pieces.
2. Body: Align the Body Stripe face to face with the Body and sew. Repeat.
3. Head: Match the Head sides and sew from the Ear slot to the Chest B.
4. Ears: For fabric Ears cut double, seam, and turn. Fold the Ear, tuck it in the Ear slot folded forward, and sew the slot closed.

5. Tail: Match the Tail Stripe to the Tail and sew. Repeat. Match the assembled Tail top with the tail bottom, sew, and turn. No stuffing is needed. Place the Tail on the Body Stripe face to face and baste.
6. Belly: Hand or machine-sew the Belly Leg darts (optional). Align the Belly Legs with the Body Legs and sew including the Tail. Leave

C to D open on one side to turn and stuff.
7. Turn, poke out the legs with a stuffing tool, and stuff the Head with fiberfill. Fill nearly full with pellets and sew closed.
8. Sew the black Eye beads in place. Embroider a black Nose or use two black beads for this. Trim the fur around Eyes and Nose.

Skunk Pattern

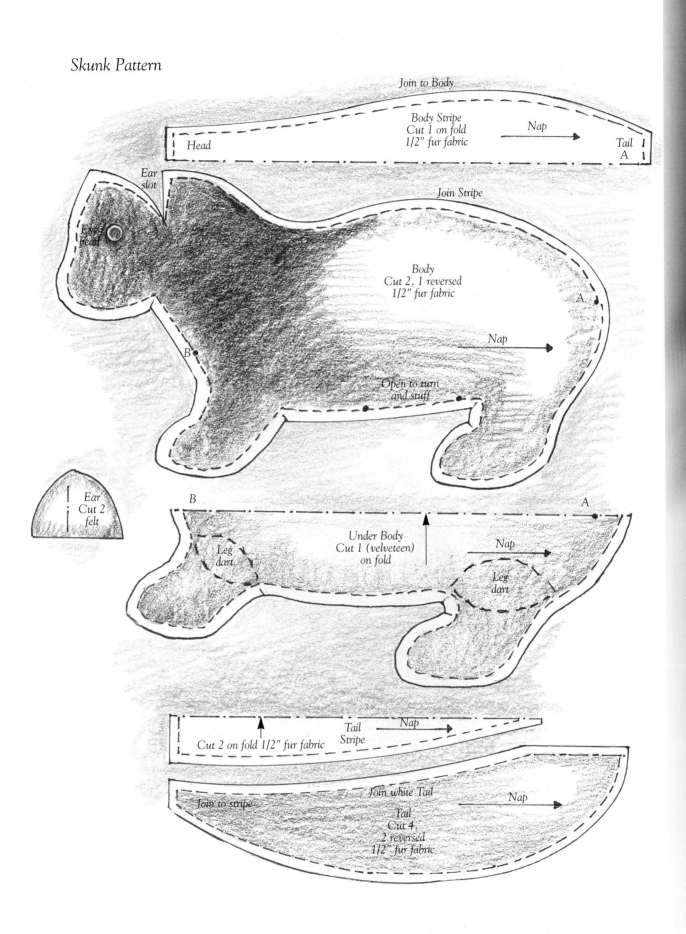

Join to Body

Body Stripe
Cut 1 on fold
1/2" fur fabric

Nap

Head

Tail
A

Ear
slot

Join Stripe

Eye
bead

Body
Cut 2, 1 reversed
1/2" fur fabric

A

Nap

B

Open to turn
and stuff

Ear
Cut 2
felt

B

A

Leg
dart

Under Body
Cut 1 (velveteen)
on fold

Nap

Leg
dart

Cut 2 on fold 1/2" fur fabric

Tail
Stripe

Nap

Join white Tail

Join to stripe

Tail
Cut 4,
2 reversed
1/2" fur fabric

Nap

39

Ringlet, the Raccoon

Makes a 6" long raccoon (plus tail).

◄ *Use a photo or an encyclopedia picture as a guide to paint details on the fur. Separate fibers that stick together with a sharp point* before the paint dries. Blend color softly to lessen the harshness of applied paint.

▲ *Noted for their etiquette 'Coons dip their food to get it wet.*

Materials

Body: 7" x 14" dark tan short pile polyester fur fabric
Belly: 4" x 6" honey-tan short pile fur fabric
Tail Stripes: 2" x 4" black fur fabric
Eye Patches: 1" x 2" dark brown felt
Eyes: Two small black beads

Ear Fronts: 1" x 2" tan felt
Matching thread
Polyester stuffing, pellet stuffing
Sewing machine or hand sewing needle, stuffing
    tool, sharp scissors, funnel

Sew in the same manner as the Skunk (page 104) with these exceptions:

1. Tail: Pieces are numbered 1 to 6, with the even numbers black and the odd numbers dark tan. Align piece 1 to 2 and seam. Continue to join black to tan to the end of the Tail. Fold the assembled Tail lengthwise, sew, and turn. Baste to the Body.

2. Head: Brush the face fur upward, place the Eye patches as marked, and sew. Match the Face sides and sew from top to Muzzle. Join the Muzzle to the Head.

3. Sew the Bodies along the back seam. Pin the Ears to the Head, sew the Head to the Body. Use acrylic paint to lighten the fur around the Eye patches, the Ear edges, and Muzzle. Brush cream color, separate clinging hairs with a knife tip. Sew on two black beads for the Nose.

4. Join the Belly pieces, leaving C to D open.

5. Ears: Make a fold in the Ear. Lay it fold forward on the Head with raw edges aligned and pin or baste. Repeat for the opposite Ear.

▲ *"God is in the details" architects are fond of quoting. You can see here how far details such as fur trimming and painting are needed to create a realistic raccoon.*

Have You Thought of This?

For a wildlife party theme, use furry creatures as napkin rings. Twist the folded napkin and lay the animal over it to secure.

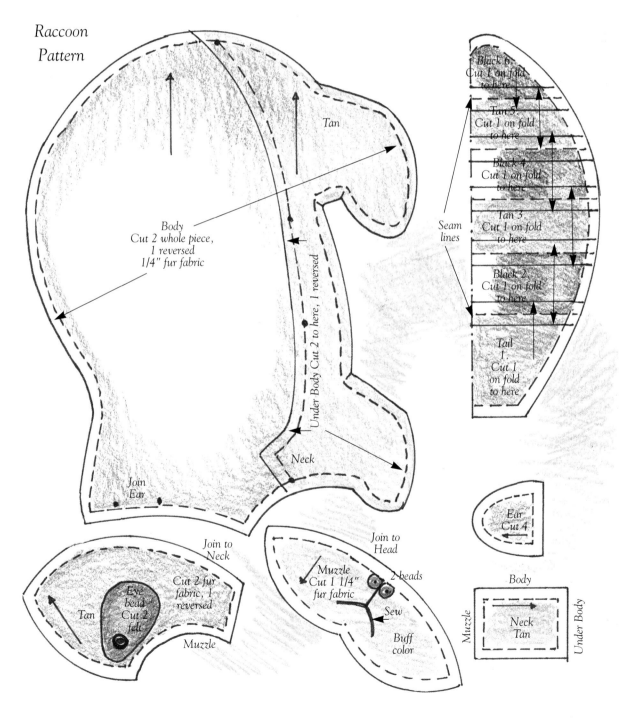

*Raccoon
Pattern*

Tan

Body
Cut 2 whole piece,
1 reversed
1/4" fur fabric

Under Body Cut 2 to here, 1 reversed

Neck

Join
Ear

Black 6.
Cut 1 on fold
to here

Tan 5.
Cut 1 on fold
to here

Black 4.
Cut 1 on fold
to here

Seam
lines

Tan 3.
Cut 1 on fold
to here

Black 2.
Cut 1 on fold
to here

Tail
1.
Cut 1
on fold
to here

Join to
Neck

Tan

Eye
bead
Cut 2
felt

Cut 2 fur
fabric, 1
reversed

Muzzle

Join to
Head

Muzzle
Cut 1 1/4"
fur fabric

2 beads

Sew

Buff
color

Ear
Cut 4

Body

Muzzle

Neck
Tan

Under Body

40

Clank, the Armadillo

Makes an 8" long armadillo (including tail). Rows of pin tucks delineate his armor.

▲ *This armored beast becomes a ball
So its feet don't show at all.*

Materials

Body: 7" x 14" honey tan robe fleece, short pile fabric, or felt
Eyes: Two small black beads
Matching thread

Polyester stuffing, pellet stuffing
Sewing machine or hand sewing needle, stuffing tool, sharp scissors, funnel

1. Pattern: (A) Before cutting the pattern pieces, mark the nine bands of pin tucking on the fabric (lines 1 cm apart). Fold the fabric on the tuck and sew nine rows. Trace the Body pattern on the pin-tucked fabric and cut out.

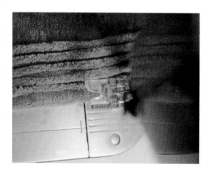

Cut out pattern pieces singly to avoid shifting. Sew on the reverse side.

2. Added pieces: (A) Ears: Fold and sew Ear pieces, sew, and turn. Repeat. Tail: Fold the Tail lengthwise, sew, and turn.

3. Body: Baste the Tail on the Body as marked. Align the Body pieces and sew from the Head to the Tail including the Tail in the seam. Match the Belly Legs with the Body Legs and sew leaving C to D open on one side. Sew the Leg darts for more upright Legs.

4. Head: Match Head sides and sew from Chin to Nose. Match Face to Head and sew.

5. Ears: Baste or pin the Ears on the Head. Turn Head right side out, tuck it in the Body Neck opening, and sew, including the Ears in this seam.

6. Turn, stuff the Head and Feet with fiberfill. Fill with pellets and sew the opening closed.

7. Sew on black bead Eyes, through the head stuffing to secure.

Armadillo Pattern

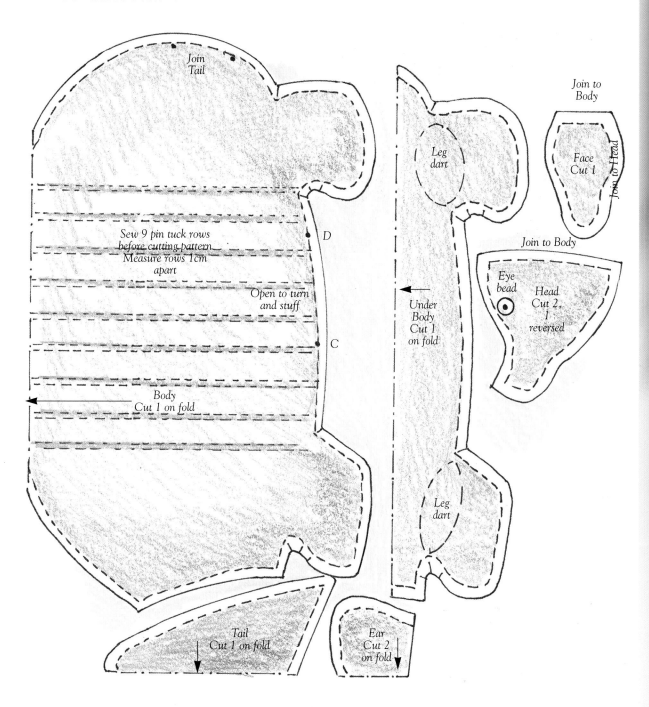

Join
Tail

Sew 9 pin tuck rows
before cutting pattern
Measure rows 1cm
apart

Open to turn
and stuff

D

C

Body
Cut 1 on fold

Tail
Cut 1 on fold

Leg
dart

Under
Body
Cut 1
on fold

Leg
dart

Ear
Cut 2
on fold

Join to
Body

Face
Cut 1

Join to Head

Join to Body

Eye
bead

Head
Cut 2,
1
reversed

41

Swirl, the Sea Otter

*Makes a 6-1/2" sea otter.
Note the way the legs are sewn.*

Have You Thought of This?

By chance, I found myself using the sea otter as a pin cushion beside my sewing machine as I made these little toys. You might like to do this, too. Fill your toy with pellets or sand, or emery for sharpening needles.

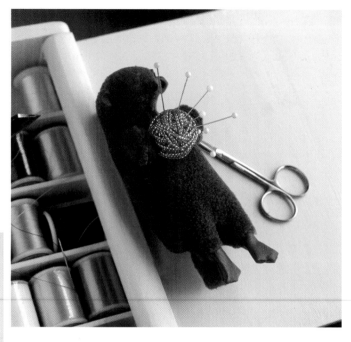

▲ *He cracks big sea shells on his tummy.
He thinks that oysters taste quite yummy.*

Materials

Body: 7" x 14" dark berber or fur fabric
Feet and Ears: 3" x 4" leatherette fabric
Eyes: Two small black beads
Matching thread

Polyester stuffing, pellet stuffing
Sewing machine or hand sewing needle, stuffing
    tool, sharp scissors, funnel

1. Pattern: Cut out the pieces singly. Sew from the reverse side.

2. Added pieces: Fold the Ear face to face, sew, and turn. Repeat. Fold the Tail lengthwise, sew, and turn.

3. Slots and darts: Tuck the Tail in the Body Tail slot and sew. Fold and sew the Body side darts. Fold the Ear, tuck it in the Ear slot fold forward, and sew. Repeat.

4. Belly: Align the Belly with the Body, matching the Back Legs. Sew from Heel to Heel. Do not sew the other Belly seams yet.

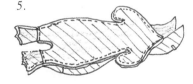

5. Web Feet: Open the Back Leg and align the Foot face to face. Sew across. Repeat.

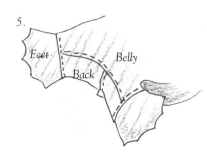

6. Body: Align the Body and Belly Legs. Fold the Back Foot and sew the Foot contours. Continue to sew up the Leg, the side, and the Front Leg to the Chin. Repeat.

7. Align the Top with the Head and sew from the Nose to the back of the Head. Repeat for the other side, leaving C to D open.

8. Turn, stuff the Head with fiberfill, and fill the Body with pellets. Sew C to D closed.

9. Face: Sew on black bead Eyes, sewing through the Head to hold the stuffing in place. Use black embroidery floss or two beads to sew the Nose. Sew Mouth as marked.

8.

9.

Sea Otter Pattern

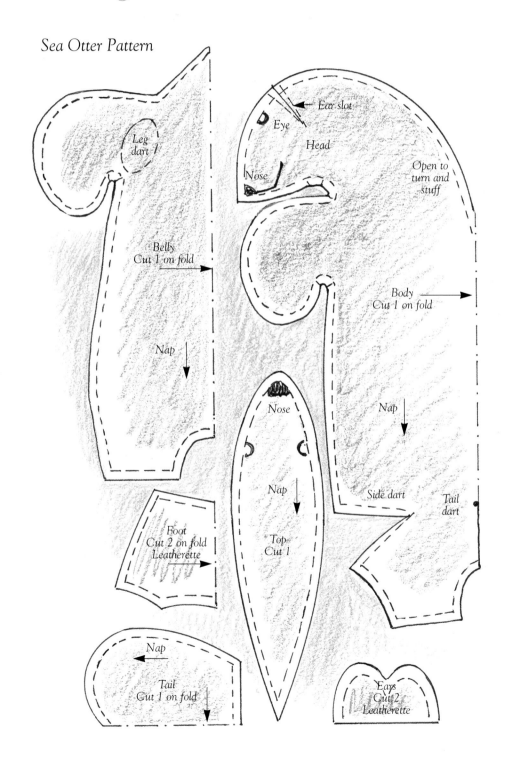

Leg dart

Ear slot

Eye

Head

Nose

Open to turn and stuff

Belly
Cut 1 on fold

Body
Cut 1 on fold

Nap

Nose

Nap

Foot
Cut 2 on fold
Leatherette

Top
Cut 1

Side dart

Tail dart

Nap

Nap

Tail
Cut 1 on fold

Ears
Cut 2
Leatherette

These toys have shifting pellets for stuffing, good for balancing on Ian Goodrich's legs.

Tips and Techniques for Designing Your Own Toys

When a pattern is provided, you can simply sew it according to directions, but if you want to make your own patterns, or know why things turn out as they do, consider these following basics of toy design and construction. Some basics are based on the rules of geometry for figuring out shapes and areas, but you don't need to know geometry to work with the few rules used. Each concept, with a toy to demonstrate it, shows how to develop your own patterns from the simplest to the more complex and describes the measuring and computing involved.

The Basics

The basic concepts that follow will help you to visualize the toy, then measure and cut the pattern pieces the sizes and shapes you need. The toy patterns given demonstrate the basics. It helps to find similar patterns throughout the book where the basics are applied. Toy patterns in this book are grouped by their construction similarities which allows you to compare pattern similarities and differences.

Have You Thought of This?
Their small size and light weight make these stuffed toy characters ideal for decorating the Christmas tree. Sew a thread loop for the wire hook, or push the hook directly through the toy's fabric.

Basic Number 1. The more you stuff a toy, or any sewn fabric shape, the rounder it gets—not squarer, not flatter, just rounder.

Stuff a fat pillow in a pillowcase and it gets rounder. Notice that a stuffed pillowcase is not as wide as a flat pillowcase, but much thicker. The fabric amount (area) is the same but the shape is different—rounder. The Eel is a good example. This sea creature begins as a simple long, flat piece of fabric, is sewn into a tube, and fills to roundness.

From this you know: That the patterns for the toys you design must be wide enough to fill to roundness the size you want.

42 Ellie, the Eel

Makes a 9" long eel; however, the fabric used stretches. After several kids and adults played with the eel, it "became" 9-1/2" long.

Materials

Body: 4" x 9" lightweight polyester knit with printed metallic design overlaid
Eyes: Two post and washer plastic Eyes, 3/8"
Matching thread
Pellet stuffing
Silk pins, sewing machine or hand sewing needle, sharp scissors, funnel, bamboo skewer

▲ *Electric eels' grins look mocking And their zap can be quite shocking.*

1. Pattern: This pattern is designed for non-fray lightweight decorative fabric to be sewn by machine and stuffed with pellets. Cut out the pattern pieces with seam allowances. Mark and cut tiny Eye insertion holes. For an unstable fabric like the one shown, trace or photocopy the pattern on paper. Fold the fabric face to face, position the paper pattern on the doubled fabric, and pin. The paper pattern acts as a stabilizer during sewing.

2. Sewing:
A. Hand sew around the Eel with a firm whip-stitch, leaving C to D opening to stuff and turn. Sew on the right side for felt, wrong side out for fabrics.
B. Machine sew on the wrong side, stitching through the pattern and stabilizing paper pattern. Set the machine to 1mm stitches, begin at C, and sew to D. Cut out the Eel 1/4" from the seam line and tear off the paper backing.

3. Insert Eyes: Before turn-

ing the Eel, insert the Eye posts and push the washers on tightly.

4. Fold the Eel flat and zigzag stitch over the fold along the spine to make a fin. Secure and clip threads ends.

5. Turning the Eel: Pull the fabrics apart on the Head and push the Nose seam into the Head and out the Belly opening. Use the blunt end of the skewer to gently push the Eel right side out.

6. Stuffing: Use the skewer to poke fiberfill into the head. Push the funnel tip into the opening and pour pellets into the Eel with the skewer.

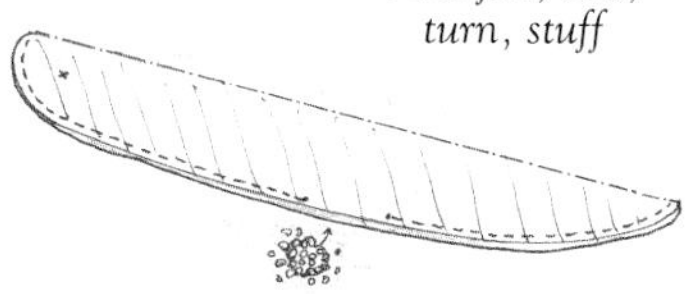

Fold flat, sew, turn, stuff

Shake the toy and work the pellets into the Tail. Stuff until full, but not bulging, until the flat Eel grows round.

7. Blind-stitch or whip-stitch the opening closed.

Eel Pattern

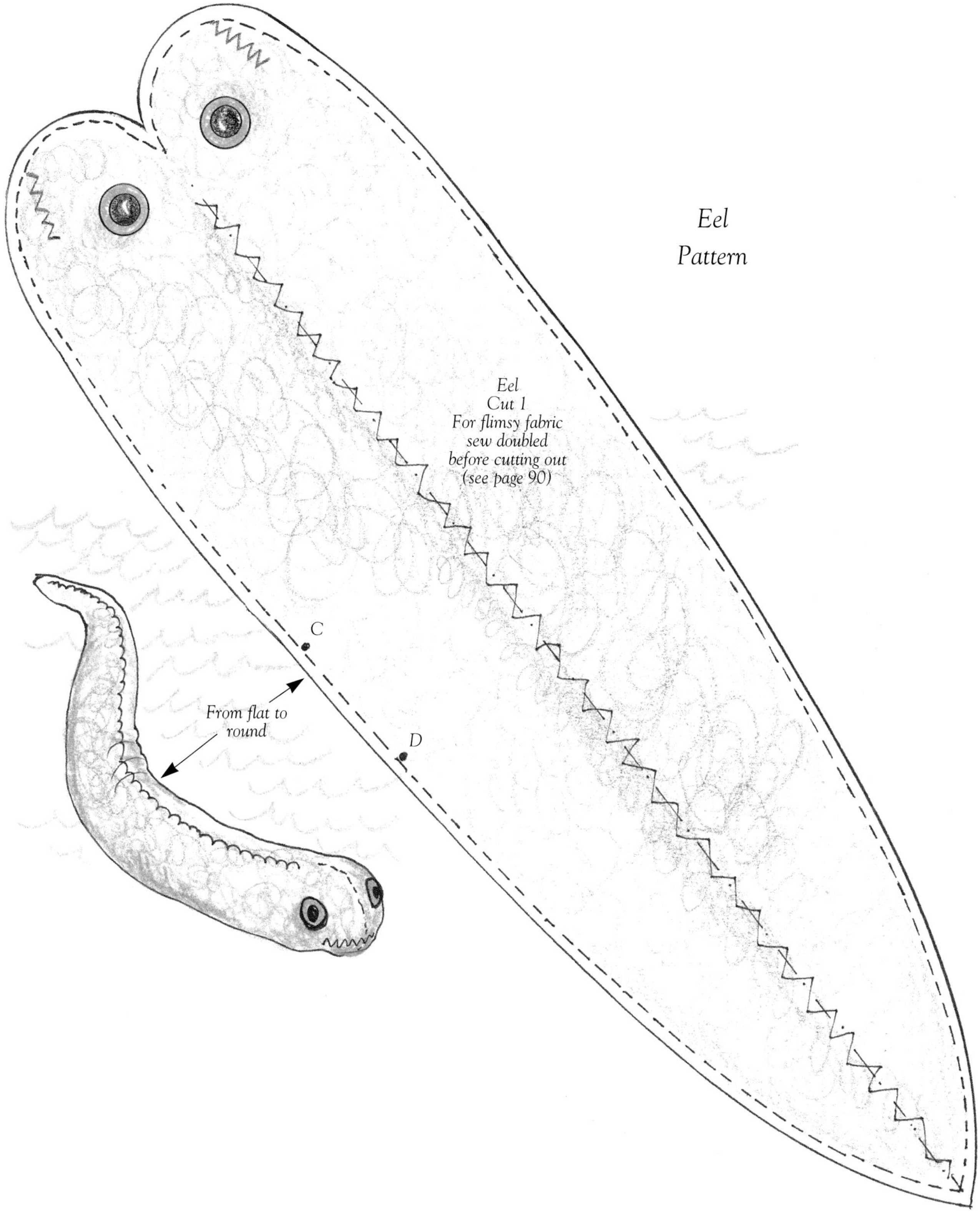

*Eel
Cut 1
For flimsy fabric
sew doubled
before cutting out
(see page 90)*

C

From flat to round

D

Basic Number 2: The outline, or distance around a stuffed shape, remains the same as when it was flat.

If you sew two round, flat pieces together and stuff them very full, the edges will wrinkle. A fat pillow in a pillowcase shows this. The rounded pillow has a shorter diameter than the flat pillowcase so the case ends wrinkle. The same happens when you sew two circles together and stuff it full: wrinkles. The small Starfish (page 21) doesn't hold enough stuffing to wrinkle at the edge, but a larger one will. Our goal is to make a fat Starfish without wrinkled edges. The most obvious way is sew darts or seams in a larger fabric to add a third dimension.

Here is a way to build in shape without adding seams. The outside edge (perimeter) must remain the same length on both pieces so the edges match. To see how the Starfish pattern developed, lay out ten tooth picks in the shape of the bottom star pattern. Now move the toothpicks so the sharp angle between the points decreases. The perimeter remains the same but the area increases as the star widens. You've added area to one without changing the perimeter, made the hill in the Starfish.

I discovered this by folding a large paper star along the peaks and valleys, aligned it to the smaller star pattern, and trimmed the edges to match. It worked!

From this you know: That pattern pieces must have joining edges (perimeter) that match in length.

43

Orion, the Big Starfish

This makes a starfish 5" across.

▲ On Orion, the big Starfish, side seams are outlined in toothpicks. When the angle of the toothpicks widens, the overall area increases, but the perimeter remains the same.

▲ While planets twinkle overhead Starfish sprinkle the ocean bed.

▶ The outline of the Starfish shape in toothpicks shows the length of each side seam.

▶ The fabric area increases when the angles between the toothpicks lessens, but the perimeter—the length of the side seams—remains the same.

Materials

6" x 12" felt or other similar fabric
Fiberfill stuffing or pellets
Matching or decorative thread

Sewing machine or hand sewing needle, bamboo
skewer, sharp scissors, funnel

For machine sewing:

1. Pattern: Cut out the pattern pieces as is or add 1/8" seam allowances for machine sewing.

2. Designs for larger Upper Star: Mark with removable

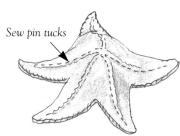

Sew pin tucks

markings where the pin tucks are sewn. Fold on these lines and hand or machine sew pin tucks from the center to the edges.

3. Edges: Align the Upper and Under Star edges and sew with a firm whip-stitch, leaving an opening to stuff and turn. Sew on the right side for felt or the reverse side for fabric.

4. Trimming: For machine-

sewn pieces, clip seam allowances on inside corners.

5. Turn: Pull the fabrics apart on one Arm. Use the blunt end of the skewer to push the Arm through the opening. Use the skewer to gently push the Arms right side out.

6. Stuffing: Poke fiberfill into each arm or pour pellets into toy. Whip-stitch the opening closed.

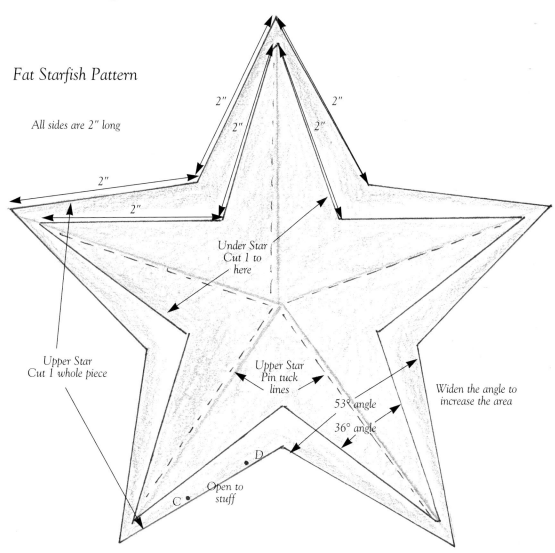

Fat Starfish Pattern

All sides are 2" long

2" 2"

2" 2" 2" 2"

2"

Under Star
Cut 1 to
here

Upper Star
Cut 1 whole piece

Upper Star
Pin tuck
lines

53° angle

36° angle

Widen the angle to
increase the area

•D

•C Open to
stuff

Basic Number 3: The distance around a round object can be computed with the mathematical formula pi, 3.14.

Making the Eel (page 114) is the easiest way to sew a three-dimensional toy: sew a long tube with closed ends and fill it. Patterns get more complicated as the toy curves in more directions. Here's an easy way to make a three-dimensional toy without adding more seams: gather a circle into a ball.

A circle is just over three times as far around as it is across. To compute how large a circle of fabric you will need to make a gathered ball, measure across your drawing. This is the diameter of the circle. Use a small calculator to multiply this by pi, 3.14. This is the circumference.

This basic formula works backwards too. To determine what sized ball a circle of fabric will make, measure across the circle and divide by 3.14. A 6" circle will make a ball 1.9" across.

From this you know: That you can compute the circumference of any roundly stuffed toy part, and the distance across the pattern pieces, by multiplying its width by 3.14.

Sting, the Jellyfish

This makes a 2-3/4" jellyfish with 9" tails.

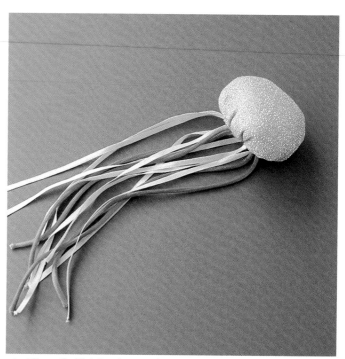

▲ *This jelly blob has hanging strings That can deliver painful stings.*

◄ *The jellyfish tails blow in the breeze in Emily Goodrich's hand.*

► *This view of the Jellyfish bottom shows gathers.*

44

Materials

6" x 6" peach-colored decorative polyester metallic
  knitted fabric
48" of 1/8" wide peach ribbon
24" of 1/8" wide orange ribbon

Thread
Fiberfill stuffing
Needle or sewing machine, stuffing tool

Pattern: Use the pattern given, or make your own. Use a compass to draw a 6" circle, or the size you want. Cut out the piece. Cut the ribbons into 12" pieces (six pieces).

Sewing the toy:

1. Sew around the edge of the circle with 3/8" long stitches or sewing machine stitches long enough to gather. For a stable fabric, sew in 1/8". For one that might pull out or fray, sew in 1/4" from the edge. Leave long trailing threads.

2. Pull the gathering thread tightly to gather it into a circle.

3. Fill the toy lightly with fiberfill stuffing.

4. Thread the gathering thread on a needle and stitch across the opening several times to secure. Fold the ribbons and sew them to the gathers.

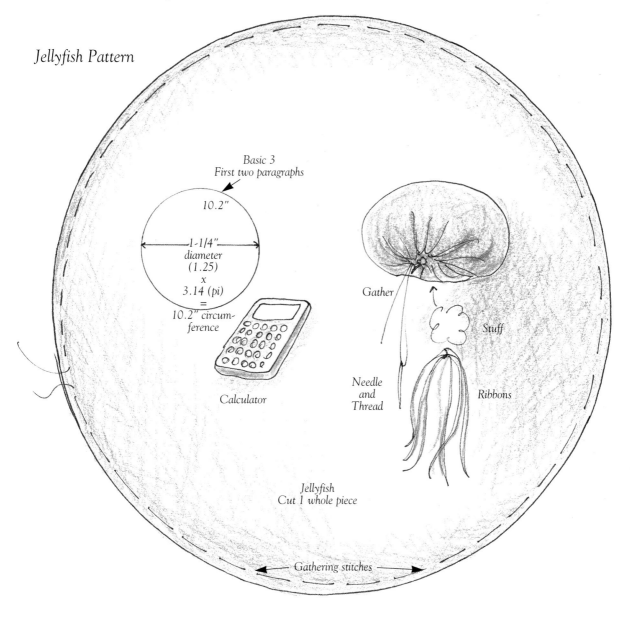

Jellyfish Pattern

Basic 3
First two paragraphs

10.2"

1-1/4"
diameter
(1.25)
x
3.14 (pi)
=
10.2" circum-
ference

Calculator

Gather

Stuff

*Needle
and
Thread*

Ribbons

*Jellyfish
Cut 1 whole piece*

Gathering stitches

Basic Number 4: Stuffed toys consist of basic geometric shapes (balls, tubes, and cones) joined.

This Mushroom pattern is a ball, tube, and circle combined. The Jellyfish (page 119) shows how to make a gathered circle, and the Eel pattern (page 115) tells you how to make a round tube. A cross-section of a tube is a circle. Slice a carrot into little pieces: first an orange tube, next a pile of carrot circles. The distance across a carrot slice—across a tube—is called the diameter. The diameter of a tube is the width of the circle needed to fill the end. Its circumference will measure 3.14 times this measure.

Boring and simple geometry, you might mutter, but measuring cuts down on Basic Number 11, the trial and error technique of cutting a pattern—or choosing clothes. Hold up a garment on a hanger and it might cover all of you in the mirror. That's your diameter, the garment's flat dimension. Try it on and squeeze time! You must hold the garment half way around yourself to see if you can get into it—diameter to diameter.

This easy-to-make Mushroom shows you how it works.

From this you know: How to measure and compute three geometric shapes, a ball, a tube, and a circle, and how to join them by matching perimeters.

45 *Bello, the* Mushroom

This makes a 2-1/2" tall mushroom.

Materials

Fabric to fit your pattern. After you've made the pattern, lay your pattern out on paper or fabric and measure how much will be needed. Use tan, gray, white, or pink felt.
Threads to match
Fiberfill stuffing and pellets
Paper, pencil, ruler, compass or string, stuffing tool

▲ *The mushroom is a type of fungus*
That scatters spores like dust among us.

◄ *"Climb up my trunk," says Mister Tree*
"The view from here is great to see."

◄ *Hattie Stroud, my granddaughter, designed this tree made like the Mushroom. From a 5" circle of Darice Foamie plastic she cut palm leaves and glued the center to a 1" x 5" felt tube trunk.*

Pattern: Make your own.

A. Make a drawing of the Mushroom or trace this one.

B. Stem: Measure across the Mushroom Stem and multiply by 3.14. Draw a horizontal line this long. Measure the height of the Stem. Draw vertical lines at each end of the horizontal one to make a rectangle this high. This is the stem pattern.

C. Stem Base: Measure across the Stem and draw a line this long. Use a compass to make a circle as wide as the line. The circle is the Base pattern.

D. Top: Measure across the Top and multiply by 3.14. Draw a line this long. Subtract the diameter of the Stem, then add the gathered seam allowances from this line. Make a circle this wide for the pattern for the Top.

E. Seam allowances must be added for other fabric because the width of the seam allowances will be subtracted from your dimensions. As narrow as 1/8" will do for non-fray fabrics, but clothing patterns commonly call for 5/8".

Sewing the toy:

1. Stem: Fold the Stem and sew the side seams top to bottom.

2. Top: Sew around the Top circle with 3/8" long stitches or sewing machine stitches long enough to gather. Leave the long trailing threads. Pull the gathering thread tightly to gather it into a circle size of the Stem.

3. Join the Stem to the Top. The best results come from sewing this part of the toy wrong side out. Tuck the gathered Top into the Stem and align raw edges. Whip-stitch the edges with a firm stitch. Turn right side out.

4. Base: Fit the Base to the Stem. Whip-stitch around the Base to join, leaving 3/4" open to stuff.

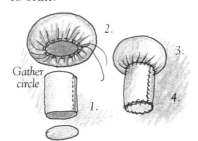

5. Stuff the Top with fiber-fill. Fill the base with pellets. Why? Pellets are heavier and will sift to the bottom. The pellets will weight the narrow base.

6. Finish sewing Base on.

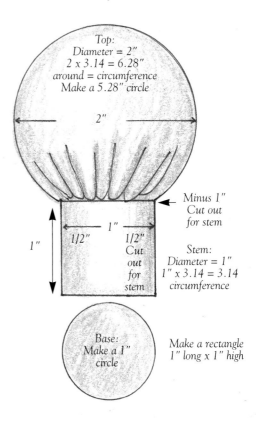

Basic Number 5: Toy shapes that curve in more than one direction like a ball need more pattern seams.

The gathered ball is not a perfect sphere. To make a rounder ball you need pattern pieces that curve more to eliminate gathers and use less surface fabric. At the playground, you'll see balls made in sections in a variety of ways: footballs or beach balls made with ellipses, baseballs made with two intersecting barbell pieces, and soccer balls made with pentagons.

What shape are beach ball sections? A good way to see this is to cut an orange into six sections. Remove the fruit and spread out the skin flat. The skin is an ellipse. The pattern pieces will be ellipses, pieces curved on each side that come to a point at the end. The length of the slice—the ellipse—will be one half the distance around the orange. You can measure and compute this shape.

Double-curved Circle Math: Here's the math for figuring areas.

1. Using a compass, draw a circle the size ball you want.
2. Multiply the circle width (diameter) by 3.14 for the distance around.
3. Draw a base line one half the circumference (distance around the circle) or measure from tip to tip on the orange skin.

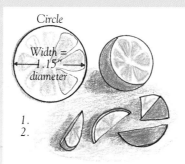

Circle
Width = 1.15" diameter

1.
2.

4. Divide this distance around by the even number of pattern pieces you plan to use. The answer is the width of the pattern pieces. Choose six for a good compromise. A stiff fabric ball will need more seams, stretchy fabric fewer.
5. In the center of the base line (Step 3), measure up half of the answer (Step 4) and place a mark. Measure down half the distance and make a matching mark. This is the width of the pattern piece (orange peel).
6. Use a compass to arc from the end of the base line, through the mark in the center, to the other end of the base line. Make the same arc below the base line. You've created an ellipse... or a perfect orange peel pattern.

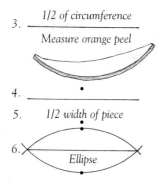

3. _____
1/2 of circumference

Measure orange peel

4. _____ •

5. 1/2 width of piece •

6. Ellipse

7. Cut out six of these pieces and sew the edges together to make a ball. Leave an opening to turn and fill the ball with fiber-fill for roundness or with pellets for a heavier ball.

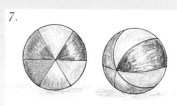

7.

From this you know: How to achieve a ball or double-curved shape without the wrinkles produced by gathering.

Why Choose Six Sections? Four sections make a squarish ball. If the fabric is very flexible and stuffed very full, the ball will be round but the seams may wrinkle. (Read about the Starfish, page 116.) To check this, make this shape ellipse and measure the length of the arc with a tape measure. The six-piece ball's arc is closer to the right length.

Toy pieces often need pattern pieces shaped like a section of orange peel, like the Owl's head (page 76) and the Dachshund's back end (page 102). The Puffer Fish is the roundest creature I could find for you to try this pattern concept.

Maximus, the Puffer Fish

This makes a 5" fish.

▲ *The puffer fish is commonly small.
When scared he puffs into a ball.*

◄ *Robbie Hueter says you must handle a real puffer fish very
carefully because of its prickly spines. Robbie's dad does research
on care of sharks at Mote Marine in Sarasota, Florida.*

Materials

Fish Body: 8" x 16" decorative fabric
Eye: Post and washer plastic Eye
Thread to match
Fiberfill stuffing and pellets
Sharp scissors, stuffing tool, paper, pencil, ruler, compass or
   string

Pattern: Make your own or check dimensions on the
pattern given.

Pattern piece A. Use the drawing of the Puffer to
measure. To compute the ball part of the Puffer, measure across the fish. Multiply this by 3.14 for the distance around. Divide this in half for the length of the
fish. Divide the distance around by 6 for the width of
the pattern pieces. Draw the ellipse pattern piece. Cut
two in fabric for the Puffer Fish sides.
Pattern piece B. For the Tail the pattern piece needs
extending. The Puffer's tail is fairly flat so the pieces
must narrow to this width. An end view helps to see
what's going on.

1. Draw the Puffer's Body circle and draw three diameter lines across it that intersect in the center. This is the Fish's Nose end.

2. For the Tail end, measure across the Tail where it joins the Body and make a smaller circle within the first this size.

3. Because the Tail is quite flat, you can trace the Tail outline from the small circle for the pattern. Rather than make the Tail in six pieces, plan to end the side pattern piece at the tail and build the tail shape into the other four pieces.

4. Multiply the Tail circle width (Step 2) by 3.14 and divide this by 4, the Tail pieces. This is the width of each Tail piece at this point. Add half of the Tail outline to each of the four pieces.

Pattern piece C. Trace the Fin on the Fish side. Draw a straight line on one side for a fold and add seam allowances to the other edges.

Seam Allowances: The above felt pattern has no seam allowances. To sew the shape from another fabric from the reverse side, you need to add seam allowances because this amount of material will be subtracted from your dimensions. Seam allowances for a stable fabric can be as narrow as 1/8". For one that might pull out or fray, sew in 1/4" from the edge.

Sewing the Toy:

1. Fins: Fold the Fin face to face and sew the edges. Turn and tuck the ends in the width of the seam allowance 1/8". Pin the Fin on Body piece A and top-stitch or satin stitch in place. Repeat for the Fin on the other Body A.

2. For a post Eye, mark and clip the Eye slit on Body A. For an appliqué Eye, sew the Eye on at this time.

3. Body: Align two (one reversed) pattern B pieces and sew along the Fin side to the end of the Tail. Repeat for the other side. Align Body A with Body B and sew from the Nose to the Tail joining. Repeat for all four seams. On the last seam, leave open for 3/4" to turn and stuff.

4. Insert the Eye post and push the washer firmly on the post. Turn the Puffer right side out.

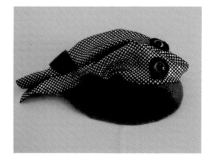

5. Stuff the Top with fiberfill or pellets. If you stuff with pellets, the fish will flatten along the bottom.

6. Sew the opening closed.

Puffer Fish Pattern

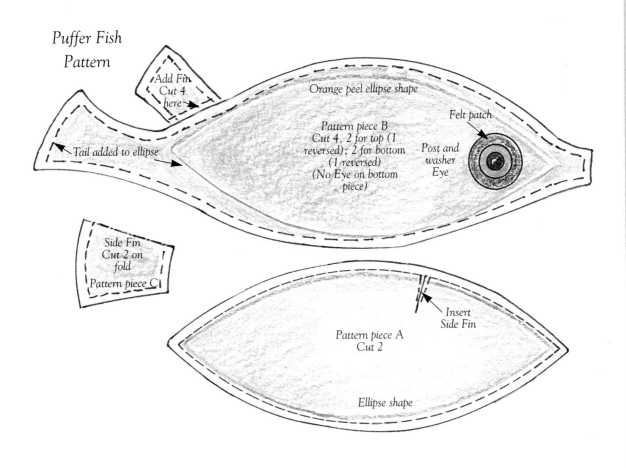

Add Fin
Cut 4
here

Orange peel ellipse shape

Pattern piece B
Cut 4, 2 for top (1
reversed); 2 for bottom
(1 reversed)
(No Eye on bottom
piece)

Felt patch

Post and
washer
Eye

Tail added to ellipse

Side Fin
Cut 2 on
fold

Pattern piece C

Insert
Side Fin

Pattern piece A
Cut 2

Ellipse shape

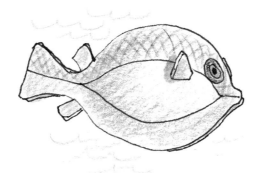

Basketball-shaped
puffer fish

Basic Number 6: A person or animal shape can be analyzed for basic geometric shapes to plan construction.

Toys are made from variations on basic shapes. The Mole pattern is made up of a tube body, a ball-shaped back end, and a cone-shaped head and tail. You know how to measure and make a tube (the Eel, page 114) and a ball (the Puffer Fish, page 123). A cone at the base is a circle. To measure the perimeter of the base, measure across it and multiply by 3.14. This is the length of the cone edge. The cone height is the same length all around, the radius. The pattern for a cone is part of a circle. To test this, fold a paper circle in half and join the folded edges. You made a cone. Overlap the fold and the cone is thinner.

The Mole's tail is a long, skinny cone. The Mole's head is also a cone, but made in three sections since it is attached to three body sections. The Mole's back end is ball-shaped. Instead of six sec-

tions (page 122) this area has three ellipse-shaped pieces (two sides and the belly). Analyze some of the other toys in this book to see what basic shapes are there and how you might make them.

From this you know: How to go about analyzing a toy you plan to construct as to basic shapes. And you know how to measure and make basic shapes.

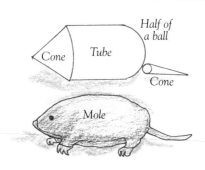

Velvet, the Mole

This makes a 7" long mole (including tail). This pattern is designed for a short pile fur fabric to be sewn by machine on the reverse side with hand-sewn details. The feet are felt whip-stitched on the right side to avoid the need to turn.

▲ *Moles make tunnels underground
So grubs watch out when they're around.*

Materials

Body: 9" x 9" gray-brown berber cloth, felt, or short
    pile polyester fur fabric
Tail: 2" x 2-1/2" gray-brown suede cloth
Nose and Feet: 2" x 5" pink or natural felt
Eyes: Two small black beads

Matching thread, pink and dark brown
Pellets
Sewing machine or hand sewing needle, stuffing
    tool, sharp scissors, funnel

1. Pattern: Cut out each piece singly so the pattern won't shift.

2. Added pieces: Fold the Tail fold and sew the length of this cone-shaped piece. Turn and stuff minimally with pellets. Pin the top closed until joining.

3. Body: Sew the Feet on the Body Legs, matching raw edges. Baste the Tail at the back end with raw edges matching. Align the Body Pieces and sew from the back end B to the Nose, including the Tail in this seam.

4. Nose: Align the Nose with the Body and sew across.

5. Head: Match the Belly with the Body at the Legs and Nose. Fold the Nose to align and begin to stitch at the Nose. Sew the Body excluding the Feet to the Tail. Continue to sew the second side, leaving C to D open, ending at the Nose.

4.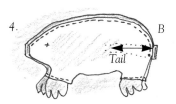

5.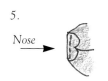

Nose

Sew Feet

5.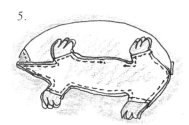

6. Sew the felt Feet by hand.

7. Turn and fill with pellets. Whipstitch the opening closed.

8. Finish: Sew two black Eye beads into the Head.

6.

Mole Pattern

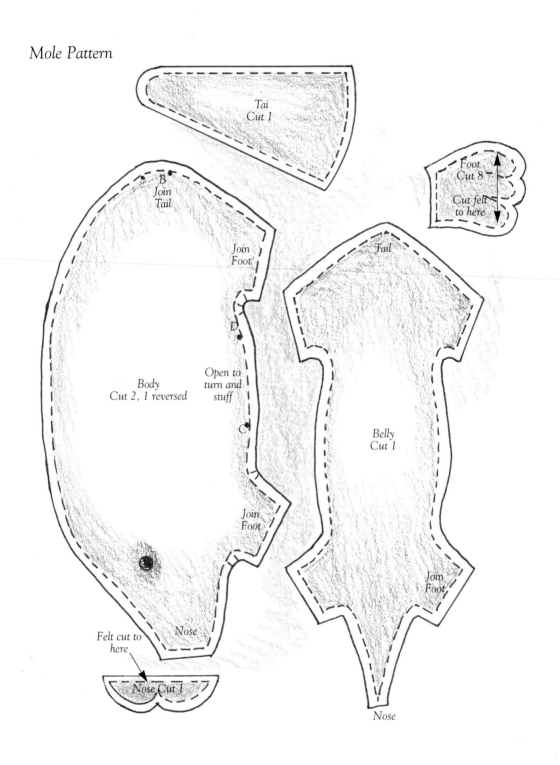

Tail
Cut 1

Foot
Cut 8

Cut felt
to here

B
Join
Tail

Join
Foot

Tail

D

Body
Cut 2, 1 reversed

Open to
turn and
stuff

Belly
Cut 1

C

Join
Foot

Join
Foot

Nose

Felt cut to
here

Nose Cut 1

Nose

Basic Number 7: Three views are useful to draft pattern shapes and decide on seam placement.

How to Make a 3-D Pattern from a Drawing

You need to decide how to make shapes and where to put seams when designing a toy in order to make a pattern. Three views of an object are often necessary to see dimensions and relationships. Your goal is to make three drawings like house floor plans. A front view, side view, and top view can show the necessary dimensions and shapes. You can use a few simple drafting tools and techniques to draw these views.

Tools and materials needed:

Pencil
Paper
Ruler
Triangle
T-square (handy but optional)

Steps It Took to Design a Ladybug Toy

Simplify: If you know enough about the toy animal you plan to make you can draw these three views based on one view. I've watched ladybugs make their tiny way across my hand enough times to know they are round on top and flat on the bottom. They have six legs tucked under that flat bottom. The head is actually a thorax and head together that looks like one head.

1. Top View: Draw a straight forward view of the object. For a Ladybug, it is a top view. Simplified, the Ladybug consists of two overlapping circles. To draw this, tape paper to a flat surface near a straight edge and draw a base line on paper at right angles to the edge using the T-square along the straight edge. Or use the ruler for a straight line and the triangle aligned on it for a right angle.

2. Side view: Draw two overlapping half circles for this view. Keep the T-square on the base line and draw lines down at right angles from the Ladybug tail end, neck, and head top down. Move the T-square up from the top view and draw a new base line across these vertical lines which is the length of the bug. The right-hand distance between lines is the head size. Use a compass to make a circle from the left vertical lines for the shape of the back. Make another overlapping circle for the head on the right. You can use a compass to make accurate circles or eyeball it for a thicker bug (shown).

3. End view. For this, draw a third base line across the paper to the right. For the height of the pieces, draw across from the top of the back and the top of the head. For the width, trace the Top View and line it up with the base line of View Three at a right angle (so the head is upward). Draw right angle lines from the body width and the head width up across the third base line. Draw the body circle from these intersecting lines—as wide as the top view and as high as the side view.

4. From this, shape the pieces as in Basic 5, Puffer Fish (page 123). Find a view that shows an outline of the piece at a seam. Measure along the outline from one view for the length of the piece. Measure along the outline from another view for the width, from a third view for the height.

From this you know: That the outline of a stuffed toy, whether on a drawing or from measuring the toy, is the actual length shown… no computing.

Spots, the Ladybug

This makes a 3-1/2" long ladybug.

Pattern-making materials

Calculator
Flexible curve guide
Pencil and eraser
Plain paper
Right angle triangle and T-square
Scissors
Tape measure

▲ *Wee ladybug just never rests*
As she nibbles on garden pests.

To make the pattern (details of these directions above):

1. Draw the outline of a Ladybug from the top.

For Wing base measure outline length

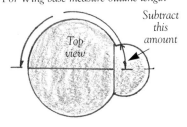

2. Using the same length of body and head, draw the profile from the side.

For Wing edge measure outline length

Measure half of outline

For Head: Measure outline of Head top view (1); Measure outline of Head side view (2), Measure outline of Head front view (3)

3. Using both of these drawings, draw the end which will also be a cross-section.

4. Draw the pattern pieces using these dimensions. You can compute these distances or measure the outline to make the pattern. Note the pieces will be shaped like a football.

Begin with top view:

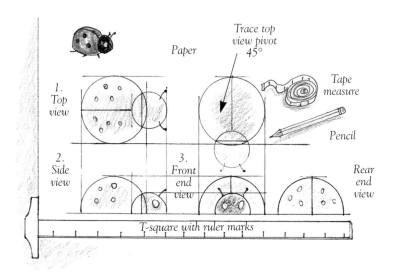

Materials

Wings: 4" x 5" red felt
Head, Body, Legs, Spots, and Feelers: 4" x
  6" black felt
Fiberfill stuffing or pellets
Black thread
Sharp scissors, sewing machine or hand nee-
  dle, stuffing tool or funnel

1. Pattern: Cut out all pattern pieces. Sew the Ladybug from the reverse side.

2. Spots: Appliqué or hand sew the spots on the Back as marked or paint or print them on.

3. Feelers and Legs: Cut a 5" x 1/4" strip for Feelers and Legs. Top-stitch four rows to secure the fibers. Clip six 1/2" legs and two 1" feelers. Baste the Feelers and Legs to the Body as shown.

4. Wings: For the back seam, straight stitch by machine and pull slightly to shorten seams, or hand whip-stitch tightly.

5. Head: Sew Head seam.

6. Assembly: Join Head to Back at the neck. Align the Back/Head section to the Body, wrong side out, with the legs and feelers tucked in. Sew from C to D all around the Ladybug. Turn and gently pull the seams open.

7. Stuff the Ladybug with pellets or fiberfill. Sew C to D closed.

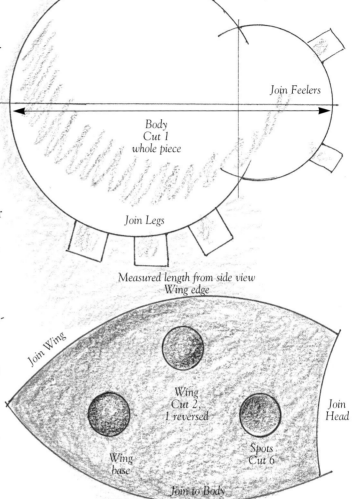

Ladybug Pattern

Join Legs

Join Feelers

Body
Cut 1
whole piece

Join Legs

Measured length from side view
Wing edge

Join Wing

Wing
Cut 2,
1 reversed

Join
Head

Wing
base

Spots
Cut 6

Join to Body

Measured length from top view

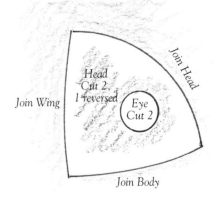

Join Wing

Head
Cut 2,
1 reversed

Eye
Cut 2

Join Head

Join Body

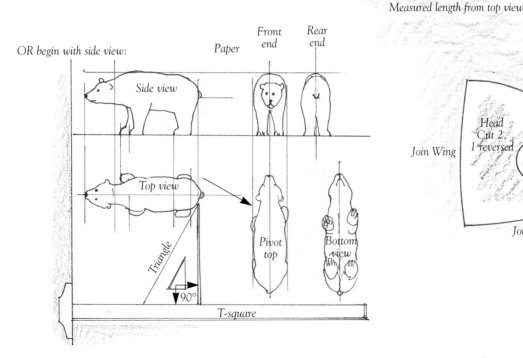

OR begin with side view:

Paper

Front end

Rear end

Side view

Top view

Pivot top

Bottom view

Triangle

90°

T-square

Basic Number 8: Photos of a model help define details for accuracy.

The Ladybug (page 130) was made in a technical way with three different views drafted to calculate and measure dimensions to create pattern pieces. Because you know how this works, you can avoid going through all of these steps in detail and work from a photograph.

My grandson Bradley took this photo of a great blue heron that lives on the pond. Bradley waited until he got a side view that shows the bird's shape most clearly. From this, it is possible to measure and calculate to make the pattern pieces.

To make a pattern from a photo, you need a simple calculator, ruler or tape measure, paper and pencil, and a photo or picture of the animal you plan to make.

First, decide what size you want. If you plan to make a 7" tall Heron, you can photocopy the photograph to that size. Another way is trace the bird outlines on graph paper and scale up mathematically. To make a 4" tall bird 7" tall, divide the height you want (7") by the height of the drawing (4"). From this you know that 1" on the tracing paper equals 1-3/4" on the 7" bird.

Make a sketch to analyze the basic shapes of your bird or animal (Fig. A). You know how to make each of these shapes, so now you want to know the dimensions. Draw a mid line down the center of the bird tracing (it will curve) (Fig. B). Measure across the bird at the widest place. Multiply this distance by 3.14 to determine the circumference there. Divide this in half for each side of the bird for the pattern width. At the widest place, add half of the width on one side of the line and half on the other at right angles to the mid line. Continue to measure across the tracing at various places and calculate the width: multiply the measurement by 3.14 for the circumference and divide in half for the width. Divide each width in half and make marks at right angles to the mid line. The result will be a dot pattern circling the bird tracing.

Draw a line from one dot to another. Some of the lines will cross, particularly at the neck. Plan to make a seam here. Measure the traced bird outline and compare it to the dot to dot line (Fig. C). If the dot line is longer or crosses another line, you will need to reduce the length by reconfiguring the pattern piece, making a dart, or by placing a seam here.

To determine where these seams will go, note where the color changes are on the bird; these are the best places to make less visible seams (Fig. D). Consider the shape of the orange peels in Basic Number Five, page 123, the ellipse. Pattern pieces will most likely be fat in the middle and come to a point at the ends. Where tube-shaped pieces join ball shapes, such as the neck, a circular shape will be cut out of the point end of the pattern (Fig. E).

The neck will have overlapping dots and gaps between dots when you measure the outline and compare to the outline measurements. The varying distance will make the neck curve more or less depending on the distances. To experiment, make a neck with the curves as traced and then one with the distances computed to see what happens.

When the model is complicated, analyze the model in terms of balls, cones, and tubes. You know how to compute these areas. Apply this to the bird pattern.

From this you know: How to create specific pattern pieces based on geometry and knowledge of how to make the basic shapes.

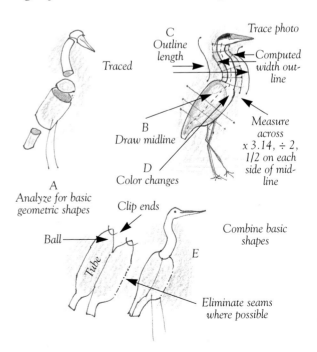

Traced

Trace photo

C
Outline length

Computed width outline

B
Draw midline

Measure across
x 3.14, ÷ 2,
1/2 on each side of mid line

D
Color changes

A
Analyze for basic geometric shapes

Clip ends

Ball

Tube

Combine basic shapes

E

Eliminate seams where possible

49

Stalks, the Great Blue Heron

This makes a 7" tall heron. This pattern is designed for an assortment of fabrics, including felt or flat fabric and a long pile fabric, to be sewn by hand or machine on the reverse side with hand-sewn details. The feet are pipe cleaners twisted to shape.

▲ *The Heron has a knife-like bill And great long legs for standing still.*

Materials

Wings, Tail, and Beak: 5" x 7" gray felt or short pile polyester fur fabric
Wing Top and Head Top: 1" x 3" black felt or short fur
Chest: 1-1/2" x 2" long white fur fabric
Neck: 4" x 5" white felt
Legs: Tan pipe cleaners

Eyes: Two small white and two small blue beads
Matching thread, pink and dark brown
Armature: Pipe cleaners
Fiberfill stuffing
Sewing machine or hand sewing needle, stuffing tool, sharp scissors

1. Pattern: Cut out each piece singly so the pattern won't shift. For fur fabric, make small clips from the reverse side to avoid trimming the pile. Mark the Leg joining and the Eye placement.

2. Head: Align the Crest to the Head, extra length at back, and sew. Repeat for the other side.

3. Beak: Overlay the gray Beak on the upper Beak and sew. Repeat.

4. Neck: Match the Neck pieces and sew up from the base to the Chin. Sew from the Beak tip to the Crest tip. Hand-sew the lower Beak from the right side because turning this tiny piece is too difficult. For a thinner fabric, machine sew the entire Beak. Stuff the Beak firmly.

5. Legs and Feet: Twist two pipe cleaners together to form the Legs given with the ends splayed as Toes. Leave 2" at the top for inside of the Body.

6. Chest: Fold the Chest and sew the Neck dart. Sew the Tail dart, leaving C to D open to turn and stuff. Match the Body to the Chest and sew from the Tail to the Neck. Repeat.

7. Body: Align the Neck with the Wing/Chest and sew. Align the Body edges and sew from the Tail to the Crest. Fold the Tail flat and sew across.

8. Legs: Push the pipe cleaner Legs into the body, aligning them as marked.

9. Stuff the Bird with fiberfill, beginning with small wads in the Head. Fill around the Leg tops firmly. Sew the C to D opening closed.

10. Top-stitch the Wing feather pattern and appliqué the black Shoulder on. Repeat. Hand-sew the Wings to the Body.

11. Finish: Sew on a white bead and a small blue bead for each Eye.

Heron Pattern

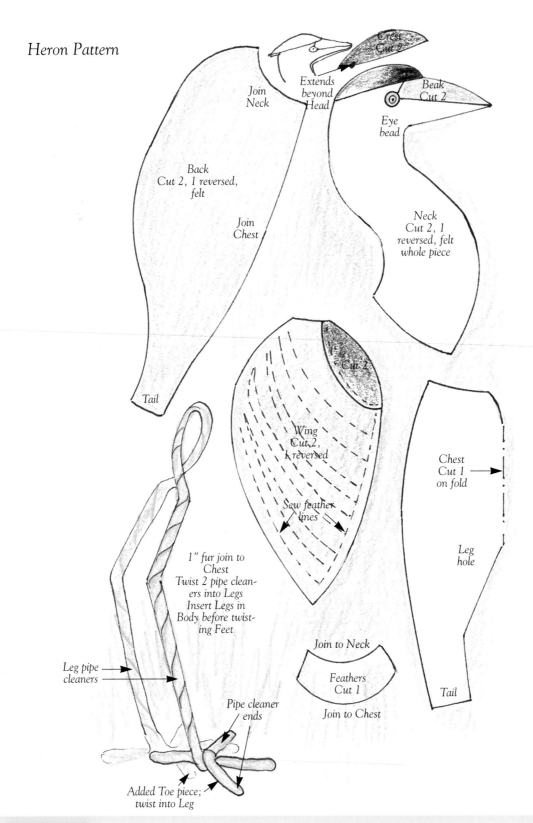

Crest
Cut 2

Extends
beyond
Head

Join
Neck

Beak
Cut 2

Eye
bead

Back
Cut 2, 1 reversed,
felt

Join
Chest

Neck
Cut 2, 1
reversed, felt
whole piece

Tail

Cut 2

Wing
Cut 2,
1 reversed

Chest
Cut 1
on fold

Leg
hole

Sew feather
lines

1" fur join to
Chest
Twist 2 pipe clean-
ers into Legs
Insert Legs in
Body before twist-
ing Feet

Join to Neck

Feathers
Cut 1

Join to Chest

Leg pipe
cleaners

Tail

Pipe cleaner
ends

Added Toe piece;
twist into Leg

Have You Thought of This?

Maybe a Great Blue Heron is not a stork, but it can be used to make the happy announcement at a baby shower. The lightweight bundle is made of paper tissue and lettered with a marking pen. To make a toy stork, choose a white body with black wing tips.

Basic Number 9: The materials used affect the design and construction of the toy.

In all the patterns, certain fabrics are suggested. Often, the material of choice is felt because it is so easy to use: it doesn't fray, cuts easily, sews easily, flexes to shape, and has a flat surface texture. Yet, it has drawbacks: it is not as sturdy as woven fabric, has limited (but wide) color range, and a flat surface texture. Like an artist searching the pallet for the right paint color, the toy maker searches the fabric store for the right fabric qualities to carry out the vision in mind. On pages 8 and 52, fabrics useful for toy making are described.

A popular fabric available is robe fleece, a soft fuzzy knitted fabric like that used for Beanie Babies. A wide range of fleece colors may be hard to find after the fall season. Fabrics are tied to fashion so their availability is limited to seasons (fleece, fur, and velvets for fall, and metallics and sequins at hol-

iday time, for example). It pays to buy short lengths of toy fabrics when you see them.

Many fur-like fabrics are produced nowadays, especially for toys. As shown on the Starfish pattern (page 21), the shape of a toy changes with the addition of a fur coat. A pattern needs to be designed thinner to compensate for this. Think about the filler when designing a toy. Will it need to be hard packed, soft, or shifting for your toy idea?

And there are ways to alter fabrics to suit the small pattern's needs and your concept. On pages 52-53, ways to alter the surface by appliqué, embroidery, or painting are explored. Described in this pattern is a way to trim fur to help shape the pattern.

From this you know: How to give your toy a hair cut to refine the shape. Trim with care; faux fur does not grow back!

Popo, the Polar Bear

This makes a 7" long bear (including tail). This pattern is designed for a short pile fur fabric to be sewn by machine on the reverse side with hand sewn details. The feet are felt whip-stitched on the reverse side, a difficult seam to sew by machine.

▲ *The polar bear likes ice and cold. His temperament is fierce and bold.*

50

Materials

Body: 9" x 9" white short pile polyester fur fabric
Feet: 4" x 4" gray felt
Ears: 1" x 1" white felt
Nose and Eyes: Four small black beads

Matching thread
Fiberfill stuffing and pellets
Sewing machine or hand sewing needle, stuffing
   tool, sharp scissors, funnel

1. Pattern: Cut out each piece singly. For fur fabric, make small clips from the reverse side to avoid trimming the pile.

2. Added pieces: Fold the Tail, sew, and turn. Baste to Body.

3. Head: Place the Ear in the Ear slot, fold the Head over it, and sew. Repeat.

4. Body: Pin the Tail on the Back end as marked. Fold the Body to align the Head and sew from the Neck A to the Tail B, including the Tail in this seam.

2., 3., 4.

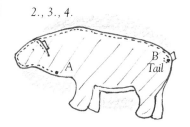

5. Belly: Sew the Leg darts now, just before turning the toy. Match the Belly pieces and sew the mid line from Chest to Tail, leaving C to D open to turn and stuff.

6. Legs: Match the Belly Legs to the Body Legs and sew from the Chest to the Tail and back to the Chest, leaving the Feet open.

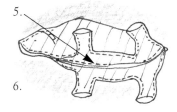

7. Feet: Align the Foot pad in the Leg opening and hand sew around the edges with matching thread. This seam is too small to sew by machine.

7., 8., 9.

8. Turn and stuff with fiber-fill and sew the opening closed.

9. Face: Use black embroidery floss to sew on back Eye beads, Nose, and Mouth as marked.

10. Trim the bear's Nose up to the ears. Trim the Legs, narrowing them to the Foot pad. Compare to the photo and trim as needed.

Polar Bear Pattern

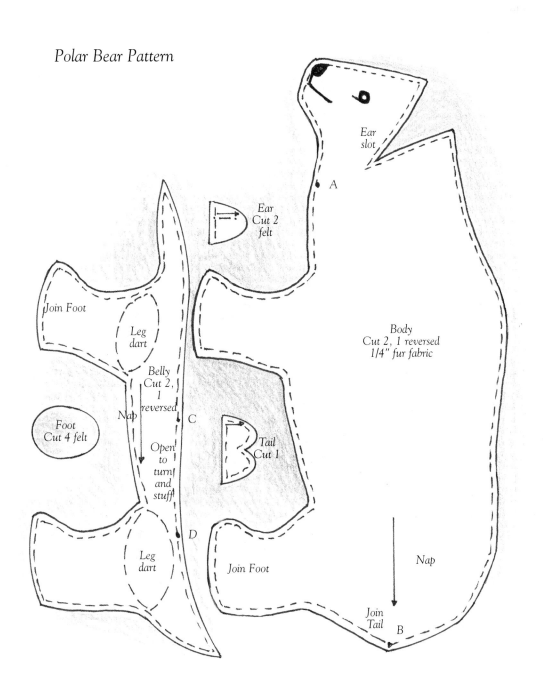

Ear slot

A

Ear
Cut 2
felt

Join Foot

Leg
dart

Belly
Cut 2,
1
reversed

Nap

C

Foot
Cut 4 felt

Open
to
turn
and
stuff

D

Leg
dart

Join Foot

Tail
Cut 1

Body
Cut 2, 1 reversed
1/4" fur fabric

Nap

Join
Tail

B

Basic Number 10: Unusual shaped toys require unusual solutions in design.

Most of the toys in the book are basically football-shaped, a long oval with rounded ends. Legs, tails, arms, heads, and horns protrude from this central shape. These toys are usually designed with seams along the mid line that run along the back and under the belly with shaping built into the ends. Some toy creatures vary considerably from this image.

The crab is one. True, a crab is somewhat football-shaped, but the body is flat horizontally and has many legs. Constructions questions come to mind. Shall the legs attach from the perimeter of the shell or should they come from underneath more true to the original? Will it be possible to actually turn and stuff all those skinny legs or shall they be sewn from felt from the right side? Maybe the legs should be sewn on doubled felt before cutting out the pattern for stability and ease of sewing?

You need to figure out inventive ways to construct the toy you plan to make. Not only should the toy show the most outstanding characteristics of the model to be recognizable, but it should be constructed in the easiest way possible with the fewest seams and the least amount of struggling to turn.

As a rule, toys are grouped in this book by the way they are constructed. The smallest felt ones with separate moveable arms and legs come first. The ones sewn all in one unit with shifting stuffing come next. You may notice that the shifting stuffing ones are larger. It is simply too difficult to make these furry toys as tiny as the felt ones; bigger is easier.

So when designing a toy, study the model and look for the basic shapes—balls, tubes, and cones, which you know how to make. Now figure how to combine and modify them into a whole toy.

From this you know: That you need to plan construction methods into designing the pattern pieces and making the toy.

Blue, the Crab

This makes a 5-1/2" wide crab. This pattern is designed for felt to be sewn by machine on the right side with hand-sewn details. The feet could be sewn on the reverse side and turned for a more authentic appearance if you are up for this much effort.

▲ *The Blue Crab's nature is quite crabby. I watch his claws for he might grab me.*

Materials

Upper Shell: 4" x 6" blue felt
Under Shell: 4" x 6" tan felt
Legs: 5" x 7" blue felt and 5" x 7" tan felt
Claws: 2" x 3" pink or flesh felt
Eyes: Four orange beads 2mm, two black beads 4mm

Matching thread, pink and dark brown
Fiberfill stuffing and pellets
Sewing machine or hand sewing needle, stuffing
  tool, sharp scissors, funnel

1. Pattern: Trace or photocopy the pattern on paper. Pin the pattern for Claw Tips and Under Shell on felt and cut them out. Pin the traced Legs pattern on doubled felt but do not cut out yet. Pin the Top Shell on felt and cut out with 1/2" seam allowances. For hand sewing, cut out all the pieces.

1.

2. Claw Tips: Fold the Claws and stitch. Turn and stuff lightly with fiberfill.

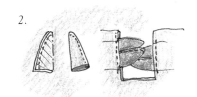

2.

3. Claws:
A. For sewing with exposed seams: On the Legs, make a stack of the paper pattern and two layers of felt and clip out the place where the Claws join only. Align a pair of Claws between the two layers at the Claw, joining within the seam lines, and sew across to join. Repeat for the other side.

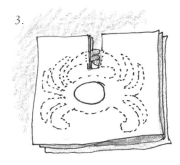

3.

B. For sewing the Legs with turned seams: Match and sew the Claw Tips on the front Legs. Sew the Legs, turn, and stuff.

4. Legs: Sew around all of the Legs. Using sharp scissors, clip 1/8" outside the seam line all around the Legs. Clip out the hole on the top of the Legs. Firmly stuff the Legs with fiberfill.

4.

5. Under Shell: Align the Legs on the Under Shell and top-stitch the Legs to the Shell. This seam closes the stuffed Legs.

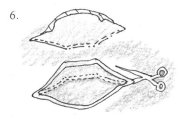

5.

6. Upper Shell: Mark the lines on the Shell top. Fold the lines in sections and pin tuck them in to make small ridges. Retrace the pattern and cut out the Shell.

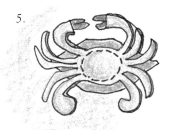

6.

7. Shells: Align the Upper and Lower Shells and sew all around. Tuck the Legs out of this seam.

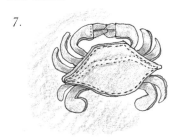

7.

8. Eyes: Sew into the Head emerging at the Eye position. Sew a knot. Sew through the orange Eye beads into the top black Bead, sew back through the other beads, and back into the Head. Pull the thread tightly and sew a knot. Repeat.

8.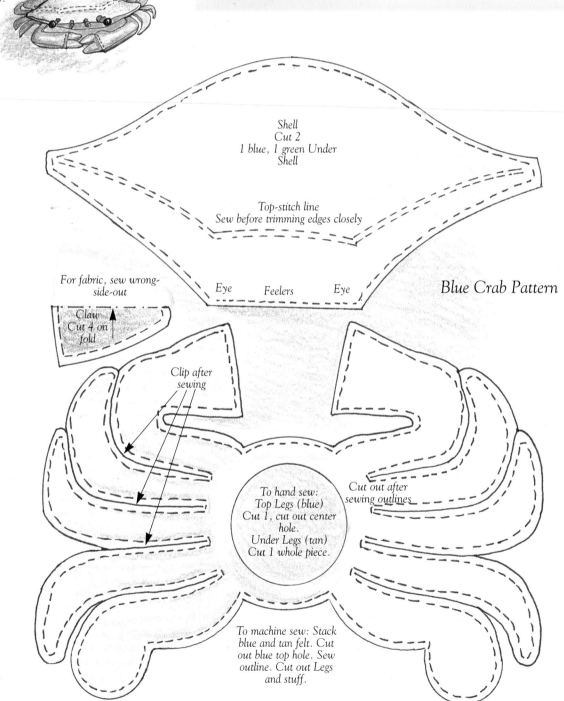

Have You Thought of This?

Soft toys sewn, pinned, or attached with Velcro onto a pillow, on curtain tie-backs, or across a curtain valance can provide a decorating theme in a flash.

Shell
Cut 2
1 blue, 1 green Under
Shell

Top-stitch line
Sew before trimming edges closely

Blue Crab Pattern

For fabric, sew wrong-side-out

Eye   Feelers   Eye

Claw
Cut 4 on fold

Clip after sewing

Cut out after sewing outlines

To hand sew:
Top Legs (blue)
Cut 1, cut out center hole.
Under Legs (tan)
Cut 1 whole piece.

To machine sew: Stack blue and tan felt. Cut out blue top hole. Sew outline. Cut out Legs and stuff.

Basic 11: When the math of patterns gets too complicated, trial and error is the way to proceed.

The trial and error technique of pattern making is called draping. Fashion designers have a body or dress form to work on, but we must simulate the form by cutting and pinning or basting the pieces together and then stuffing them to see what happens. Odd little heads and bodies in strange colors of felt are scattered all over my work table as details were worked out for patterns.

As in the garment industry, you can use all sewing techniques available: gathers, tucks, folds, easing, appliqué, embroidery, blind stitching, and more. The dragon includes a few of these so you can see the possibilities.

One of the most handy techniques is borrowing. If you see a pattern piece used for another toy, or a part of a piece the shape you need, trace it onto your pattern. Experience in sewing helps with this. The Dragon borrows from many toys: the leg of the Tyrannosaurus Rex (page 54), the neck curve of the Heron (page 132), the fabric of the Salamander (page 94), and the button joints of the Camel (page 26).

From this you know: That all of these basics are useful in designing toys and that you can augment them with the dress designer's technique of cutting and trying.

Emerald, the Dragon

This makes a 6" tall dragon (8" when standing on tip-toe). This pattern is designed with a variety of fabrics to be sewn by machine on the reverse side with hand sewn details. The feet are felt whip-stitched on the right side to avoid the need to turn.

▲ The dragon brings good luck to all.
Good sewing now from Carolyn Hall!

Materials

Body: 6" x 10" metallic fabric
Points, Ruff, and Leg Fringe: 4" x 14" pink felt
Head and Feet: 4" x 6" gold felt
Belly and Legs: 8" x 12" metallic print fabric
Eye patch: 1" x 1-1/2" green felt
Eyes and Nose: Two googly eyes*, two 4mm yellow beads

Antennas: Pink pipe cleaner
Matching thread
Fiberfill stuffing and pellets
Sewing machine or hand sewing needle, stuffing tool, sharp scissors, funnel, tailor's chalk
*This is a tiny clear plastic dome containing a shifting black eye.

1. Pattern: Cut out each piece singly so the pattern won't shift.

2. Match the Body pieces and sew the Back seam. Mark a line down the center of the points with tailor's chalk. Align the points and top-stitch the mid line to the Back seam.

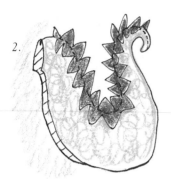

3. Match the Belly to the Back and sew from the Head to C. Repeat. Sew from D to the Tail tip.

4. Head: Match Head pieces and sew from the Nose to the Ruff and from the Nose to the Neck. Hand sew the Nose in the opening. Align the Ruffs and baste to the Head. Turn the Head right side out, tuck it into the Neck, and sew.

Head: Turn and tuck into Neck

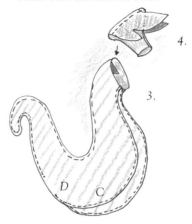

5. Turn the Body and stuff the Head and Tail with fiber-fill. Fill the Dragon firmly with pellets.

6. Legs: (See Button Joints page 26, and Sewn Joints page 27.) Match two Legs, insert the Leg fringe in the seam, and sew from Toe around to Heel. Pack the Leg with fiber-fill and hand sew the Foot to the Leg. Repeat for all Legs. Join the Legs to the Body.

7. Head: Sew two Eyebrows on each Eye. Glue the googly Eyes on. Sew on two yellow nostril beads. Embroider a black Mouth. Wrap a pipe cleaner around the Head under the Ruff, twist pieces together, and curve the ends.

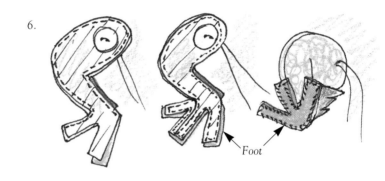

Foot

Pipe cleaner

carolyn vosburg hall '98

Dragon Pattern

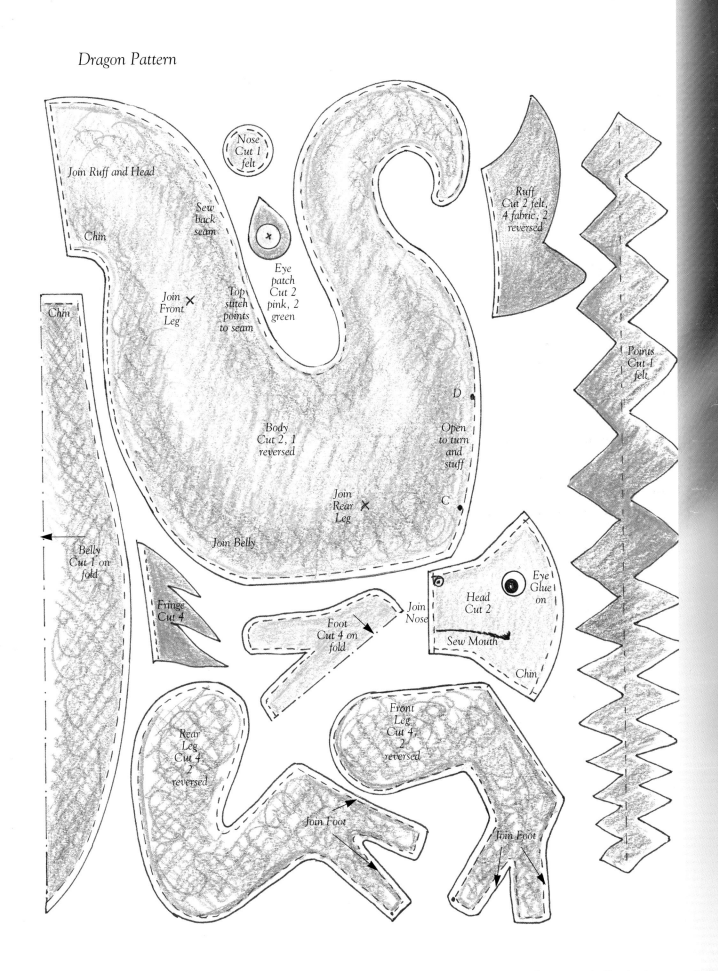

Join Ruff and Head

Chin

Nose
Cut 1
felt

Sew
back
seam

Join
Front
Leg

Top
stitch
points
to seam

Eye
patch
Cut 2
pink, 2
green

Ruff
Cut 2 felt,
4 fabric, 2
reversed

Points
Cut 1
felt

Chin

D

Body
Cut 2, 1
reversed

Open
to turn
and
stuff

Join
Rear
Leg

C

Belly
Cut 1 on
fold

Join Belly

Fringe
Cut 4

Foot
Cut 4 on
fold

Join
Nose

Head
Cut 2

Eye
Glue
on

Sew Mouth

Chin

Rear
Leg
Cut 4,
2
reversed

Front
Leg
Cut 4,
2
reversed

Join Foot

Join Foot

Join Foot

Glossary

Area: In geometry; the surface contents of any figure, such as a square, circle, or star.
Circumference: In geometry; the distance around a circle.
Compass: Tool for making accurate circles.
Diameter: In geometry; the distance across a circle (or a tube).
Ease: In sewing; to gather one edge of a piece slightly to fit another.
Fiberfill: An extruded synthetic fiber for stuffing.
Figure: A geometric shape; a circle, ball, tube, cone, etc.
Knots: In sewing; a way to secure the thread in beginning or ending stitching.
Outline: In geometry; the contour of a drawing or photo.
Perimeter: The whole outer boundary of a figure.
Pi: The ratio of the circumference of a circle to its diameter, or 3.14.
Polypropylene pellets: Plastic pellets 1/8" across used for stuffing toys.
Pipe cleaners: Chenille (short fibers) with a wire center; also called chenille stems.
Radius: The distance from the center of a circle to the edge or perimeter.
Satin-stitch: Short stitches sewn solidly to cover the fabric.
Whip-stitch: Stitching sewn over the edge (or joining edges) of fabric.

Supply Sources

Supplies and materials used in this book were purchased at the following:

Frank's Nursery and Crafts
Check your local phone directory for store information in Florida and Michigan.

Hancock Fabrics
3406 W. Main St.
Tupelo, MS 38801
Website: www.hancockfabrics.com

JoAnn Fabrics and Crafts
5555 Darrow Rd.
Hudson, OH 44236-4011
Website: www.joann.com